Myth and Today's Consciousness

Myth
and
Today's Consciousness

EAN BEGG

COVENTURE LTD
23 Chesham Street
London SW1

This edition first published in Great Britain by
Coventure Ltd., 23 Chesham Street, London SW1

ISBN 0 904575 30 6

Cover illustration: Roger Payne
Cover typography: Jutta Laing

Photoset and produced by
R James Hall Typesetting and Book Production Services
Harpenden, Herts.
Printed and bound by
Redwood Burn Ltd., Trowbridge, Wilts.

To Jennifer

Contents

Preface

THE MOVE FROM the age of Pisces into the age of Aquarius;
the end of a Platonic great year; the time for a metamorphosis of the gods.

Are these just figures of speech, or is some radical
change in consciousness really taking place which it
behoves us to recognise and accept? There is a cliché
well-known to history students that makes of every year a
period of transition.

In terms of religion the signs of transformation are clear
and striking. The Latin Mass, for instance, which for a
thousand years and more provided a common background
of experience for all Roman Catholics throughout the
world, and for which people died and killed, has been
discarded, for it seems that religion is no longer a matter of
credal assent to theological propositions or historical facts.
It is, rather, a new perception of inner, psychic potentialities whereby an individual, through greater consciousness
of the options, becomes freer to choose his or her own
way to self-realisation.

The new polytheism which is emerging is not a return
to the concretistic belief in external deities who need to be
placated, but an awareness of each person's own inner
pantheon.

If we think of the gods, in the changing world of myths,
as archetypal modes of consciousness, ways of experiencing ourselves and the world, is it not clear that an era is
coming to an end, an era of apparent consensus in which

monotheistic orthodoxy was imposed by society on its members? In what is loosely termed the Western world, pluralism is now tacitly accepted, while 'heresy' and 'orthodoxy' are terms relegated to the memory of things past. In personal choice lie the very root and meaning of the word heresy. Anyone of fifty or over today grew up in a world where standards of conduct were clearly established and subscribed to, in theory if not in practice, but today we are all heretics, nowhere more so than in the way we behave.

The image, or persona, to which it is expected one should conform in the new age, whether we call it Aquarian, post-Christian, nuclear, or space, is already revealing itself. It is both more individual and more generalised than its predecessor. The new tide runs strongly against the accidental differences that divide us, like class, nationality and religion, flowing rather with the essential qualities which unite us. Much light has been shed on the nature of these qualities by the twentieth century phenomenon of depth psychology. As a result, we are becoming more sceptical of the prophet and the hero and the guru who claims special knowledge or virtue – or at least we ought to be – and more aware of the shadow that contradicts and counteracts the aspirations of the idealist, more conscious and tolerant of the paradoxical multiplicity of human nature.

So are we all the same under the skin, subject to the same planetary powers and complexes, the same archetypal patterns of life, predictably programmed? The Saturnine voice of Aquarius would answer yes, and treat us accordingly. But the maverick magician Uranus urges us to preserve our right to unpredictability.

The true religious key-words of our age, mostly deriving from psychology, are resonant of uniqueness: individuation, self-realisation, integration, authenticity, wholeness. The paradoxical truth is that the experience of uniqueness seems to come from or with the realisation that one is not special or different, but much the same as everybody else. The gods characterise the invariables in the life of each of us, but, as is illustrated in mythology, through the experiencing of them, through the interaction of conscious and unconscious, through pondering on one's dreams and being affected by them, lies the individuation process which expresses who we really are.

The gods and their myths are mighty forces which grip the psyche; they are never more dangerous than when they are ignored, repressed or slighted. So this book is very much concerned with religion: Christianity, and the predecessors which it supplanted, and the present state of our relationship with the gods. This is a presumptuous aim which will rely heavily for its fulfilment on a subjective, intuitive assessment of the signs of the times. Particular emphasis will be placed on the need to become more conscious of the deities with whom we appear to be on bad terms. The book is unapologetically polytheistic in the same way that the circle of the horoscope contains the signs and planets and the Tarot deck its multitude of archetypal images.

For further reading on this subject, see
The New Polytheism, David L. Miller, Spring Publications, Dallas (1981) containing James Hillman's essay "Psychology: Monotheistic or Polytheistic".

Chapter 1

Metamorphosis
of the Gods

IN HIS LATE work, *The Undiscovered Self**, discussing "the
present world crisis", Jung writes of "a mood of world
destruction and world renewal that has set its mark on our
age". He goes on: "We are living in what the Greeks called
the Kairos – the right time – for a metamorphosis of the
gods, i.e. of the fundamental principles and symbols. This
peculiarity of our time, which is certainly not of our
conscious choosing, is the expression of the unconscious
man within us who is changing."

"God fulfils himself in many ways, lest one good
custom should corrupt the world" wrote Tennyson.†

New archetypal arrangements are constellated and we
must adapt to the changed influences. Blindly to oppose an
idea whose time has come is to condemn ourselves to a
hardening of the heart and mind and an ultimate crystalliz-
ing out into an empty shell of a person. Neither does it do
to succumb to unconscious possession by the new or
resurrected gods, for that is the path of the Gadarene
swine.

We have rather to understand what influences we are
under and relate them to our own individuality. At the
beginning of the Christian era, its founder rebuked the
literal-minded Pharisees for being greatly interested in

---

* p. 111, Routledge & Kegan Paul Plc, London 1958, *C.W.* Vol 10,
p. 304
† Alfred Lord Tennyson *Morte d'Arthur; The Works of Tennyson*, p. 71,
Macmillan, London 1981

forecasting tomorrow's weather and totally failing to discern the signs of the times. But at this nodal point in human history how are we to discern and understand the meaning behind appearances? Simply to look at the outward manifestations is to be bewildered.

Whether we are lost in a surfeit of sub-cultures as in the West, divorced from our roots and traditions, with no consensus beyond a grey, indifferent tolerance, or whether we are bound to the would-be rigid orthodoxy of the communist world, the problem of knowing in what ways the unknown is attempting to reveal itself is equally great.

In tribal societies, when meaning grew cold and the waters of life ceased to flow, the chief or shaman would sometimes have a big dream which could result in the establishment of a new dance or religious ritual of great importance for the psychological well-being of the tribe, which would thereby once again feel linked to the source of meaning and life. It is true that our liturgies and religious ceremonies in the Western world have undergone drastic modifications in recent years, especially the Roman rite. The somewhat iconoclastic break from the continuity of an ancient tradition is certainly a notable sign of the times, but it has not so far proved very energizing either for society or for the institutions concerned. The formal changes are the result not of a big papal dream but of the earnest labours of professional committees, a type of body that seems singularly resistant to the movements of the spirit. Vaugelas, the seventeenth century French grammarian, said that if you wanted to determine current linguistic usage you should listen, not to the lexicographers, but to the market porters of Les Halles, and the same principle holds good when it comes to determining the relative significance of new behaviour patterns. If, for example, one wishes to understand something of the spirit of an age that is past, one of the best ways of doing so is to read the imaginative literature of the period, which made the greatest impression on contemporaries.

The most striking instance is afforded by the legend of the Holy Grail, unheard of at the beginning of the twelfth century and universally known throughout Europe by the end of it. It expressed in literary form the same quest in a rough age for a healing, nourishing, civilising feminine symbol that is to be seen in the great Gothic cathedrals of Our Lady and in the cult of love to which troubadours and Cathars gave utterance in Southern France. The sixteenth and seventeenth centuries, which witnessed the increasing complexity of society, gave birth in compensation to the literature of simple, pastoral, Arcadian idylls and the idealisation of the noble savage. Romanticism and its successors sounded a contrapuntal theme to the prevailing rationalistic ethos of the new age of science by stressing the natural, the exotic and the mysterious.

A word which enters the language during the Romantic period is 'myth', first used in 1830 to denote a story involving the actions of supernatural persons or events of an earlier period. Already in classical Greek the term 'muthos' had the same sense of a legend from the time before recorded history involving gods and heroes. One could therefore apply the word 'myth' to archetypal situations taking place in what the words used to preface the reading of the Gospel during Mass refer to as "illo tempore", an unspecified time, perhaps not far from what native Australians call "the dream time".

But to use the word 'myth' in connection with the Gospels is to introduce a new element into its meaning, for Christianity relates 'muthos' (fable) to 'logos' (factual history) by situating the events of the New Testament in a precise time and place with reference to historical characters. Yet few would contradict that Christianity has also been the dominant myth of European consciousness for the last two millennia. This dominance has meant that other myths, like that of the Holy Grail, which originated in pre-Christian Celtic lore, became subsumed within the general Christian framework.

A major religious myth provides the mainspring of meaning for a whole culture. "Man does not live by bread alone" and "where there is no vision the people perish". The myth is a touchstone against which all incoming ideas are tried and tested, thereby becoming in itself a veritable mode of consciousness. But myths grow old and all pantheons experience their Götterdämmerung, albeit leaving the archetypal river-bed, however drought-stricken, a still viable channel for a renewed draught from the waters of life.

Such a latency period is also one of metamorphosis – much that has been lost or repressed during the age that is passing away re-emerges from the collective unconscious for further examination and possible reintegration. Gnosticism, a religious attitude that pervades all religions, based, not on dogma and creed, but on self-experience, was ruthlessly persecuted by the early Church to revive again and again in various forms and has never ceased to act as an alternative shadow side to conventional Christianity. Extirpated in the Paulicians, Bogomils and Cathars, it surfaced powerfully from the sixteenth century among some of the enthusiastic sects within Protestantism and has flourished since in Theosophy, Anthroposophy, and the ideas of Gurdjieff and Ouspensky, as well as in certain forms of depth psychology.

But new contents also swim into our ken from the collective unconscious, bringing fresh meaning and a transformed adaptation to the influences that play upon us as the ever-circling years usher in another age with changed archetypal configurations. It is especially at such moments, when the gods or the ancestors are apt to indicate what new arrangements are appropriate in our lifestyle or liturgy, that we need to be attentive to whatever big dreams are speaking to us. In the complicated mass-societies of the modern world it is the artist with his ear attuned to the as yet inaudible who first picks up the influences that are in the air and retransmits them to us in literature, painting and music.

One of the major themes to have been constellated in the course of this century is that of androgyny. The androgyne has always been a potent symbol of wholeness, expressing for men and women the possibility of integrating the alternative principle and choosing which mode to manifest in response to incoming impressions. Perhaps such a choice is indeed the true meaning of free will. The motif of androgyny was kept alive in Christendom by the subtleties of alchemy. More recently it became incarnated in the much derided experimental life-style associated with the Bloomsbury Group and such books as *Orlando* by Virginia Woolf. Nowadays, following in the footsteps of the troubadours, who gave expression to a new attitude to the feminine in their day, it is often the modern bards of popular music who manifest for millions, sometimes in exaggerated form, this aspect of the Zeitgeist.

In contemporary literature, no tale has more powerfully affected the hearts and minds of an era than Tolkien's *The Lord of the Rings*. From one point of view it is a wholesome epic fantasy in which good triumphs over evil. But it contains much that is peculiarly relevant to the turning-point at which we find ourselves. Ancient values, summed up in the return of Aragorn, the once and future king, to his throne, are a safeguard for whatever good may be preserved from the old order. The evil he opposes, unchanging yet novel in form, encompasses perverted science and technology within a slave state. Elements indispensable to victory include the orchestration of the free peoples by Gandalf, a Wotan/Merlin figure who launches against the common foe representatives of a race invented by Tolkien, the Hobbits. These earthy, feeling folk, whose strong sense of relatedness contrasts with the cynical rationality of the enemy are, alone among the peoples of middle-earth, relatively immune to the temptations of the power-lust, and so can be trusted to bear the baneful ring of tyranny back to the cracks of doom where it was forged. Although Frodo the Hobbit could never have put together an intergalactic communications system, he is a brother under the skin to another stranger who has found a home in the imagination of the child that lives in all of us, the little space traveller, "E.T.". For it is only with the sense of wonder and unprejudiced receptivity which characterize child-consciousness that we can relate adequately to new contacts from the collective unconscious.

The efforts of Warrior-King, Wizard and Hobbit would, however, have been in vain had it not been for the intervention of the spear-maiden, Eowyn, who, accoutred in knightly garb, slew, as a task of love, the Dark Lord of the Hosts of Mordor, whom no man could harm. Warrior maidens are not unfamiliar to us, whether their struggle is armed or peaceful, and they have a great part to play in the transformation of attitudes which no longer further the evolution of consciousness. An immediate association is presented by the exponents of the Women's Movement during the past century. Yet, amazingly, even today, the Goddess herself still speaks to us directly without necessity of art or politics. The Queen of Poland, the miraculous Black Madonna of Czestochowa, is both a work of art and a political symbol, but who can doubt that she transcends these contingent modes as the living archetypal image of a nation's true identity and self-expression, the palladium of freedom and independence against the forces of oppression and despair? Tens of thousands were aware of the potent presence of the Virgin herself at Fatima in 1917 and at Zeitoun in 1968. In this century in various places, hundreds of apparitions of the Virgin have been reported. Often her message, delivered to children or people of little education, is a sombre warning that unless a full-scale change of attitude occurs, what in religious language is called repentance, mankind faces destruction.

The turning-point is always a danger-point, when things could go either way. In terms of the astrological myth we are now in the cusp between the ages of Pisces and Aquarius. Pisces as a double sign openly posits the problem of the reconciliation of the opposites. The two fish pull against each other to find their resolution in the paradoxical mystery of Christ: man and God, born of a Virgin into time and space, yet eternally God's only-begotten, crucified between the opposites and rising into life from death. After the rough maleness of the preceding age of Aries with its military empires, Pisces needed to make known, through the law of love engraved in the heart, an other-worldly concept of kingship, and a tragic but joyful sense of life in which all are strangers and pilgrims. This was not to be. Church and State collaborated to maintain those very qualities – legalism, centralism, orthodoxy, rationality, militarism – that had been the basis of Rome's success. The feminine ideal was projected on to the symbol of the opposing sign, Virgo, and concretised as sexual abstinence, though at privileged moments like the twelfth century the beauty of holiness became manifest in the material world. But, for the most part, the Virgin remained all good, the doorway to Heaven, while the daughters of Eve were seen as all bad, limbs of Satan, ever ready to open the gates of Hell. This imbalance is now, tardily and painfully, in the process of rectification.

With the rebirth of feminine values has come an awakening of interest in the myths of meaning that are non-rational and acausal, opening on to a further dimension of consciousness. Astrology is one of these and the sense in which we are using the term 'myth' does not detract from its credibility. It offers a language of the soul, much abused, like most languages, that is imaginative, non-judgmental and, unlike most psychological jargon, non-pathologizing. Thus, when it speaks of the bisexuality or androgyny of Aquarius, it conjures up not a physical malformation or a moral deviancy but the image of a divine messenger, transcending duality, mediating two streams of radiation, gold and silver, flowing to and fro between an earthly vessel and a spiritual one.

What is evolving in step with the precession of the equinoxes seems to be nothing less than a new mode of consciousness. The very word 'consciousness', in the sense it is used today, is relatively modern and belongs to a period which was not interested in differentiating states and levels within the concept. But consciousness is not only a relative and mutable experiential condition within the individual psyche, it is a constantly shifting historical phenomenon. What a gulf, despite the thread of apparent continuity, separates the consciousness of the first three centuries of our era, still discernible in the art, literature and institutions of Rome, from that of the twelfth century! What a change in collective attitude has been experienced by anyone alive today who remembers the world before 1914!

As speech for an individual is both the product and the tool of consciousness, so the developing language of a people reflects and accelerates its separateness from others and changes in public awareness. German consciousness, linguistically moulded by a feminine sun and a masculine moon in sentences that end with verbs, full of words that stick together, is not the same as French or English consciousness.

Technology likewise affects the presuppositions which form the background of unquestioned higher generalities against which we live our lives. The consciousness of a Stone Age tribal survivor of our technological age in Amazonia or the Philippines is qualitatively different from that of a computer expert in New York, though each is programmed by the same basic drives. The Aborigines could not fit Captain Cook's ships within their scheme of things, so they acted as though they did not exist. Primitive people shown photographs of themselves for the first time seem to see nothing. Perhaps we could say by analogy that if we fail to see ghosts, auras, fairies, apparitions of the Virgin and meaning in dreams it is not necessarily because they are not in some sense real, but because our consciousness, conditioned by expectation, is not attuned to them. New symbolic representations in literature and the arts prepare the way for the ideas whose time has come which will transform the consciousness of the age, making the hitherto invisible visible.

At this juncture of revolutionary technological and socio-economic change, in which even language is bursting at the seams of vocabulary and syntax to accommodate all that is new, to what shifts in the archetypal balance of power must we be especially sensitive if we are to change profitably with the times? We had better try to recognise and integrate the contents that are struggling to emerge before they destroy us.

Thus, in *The Lord of the Rings* Gandalf's shadow-side is represented by the renegade Wizard, Saruman, who conceals his craving for hegemony beneath a veneer of eloquent plausibility that makes all hasten to agree with him. In him we learn to recognize the clerks who would betray us with sweet reason to the forces of irrational violence. Twice in our century, the old god of Sturm und Drang has erupted from his fastness in the most culturally advanced country in Europe to wreak vengeance for ancient wrongs denying Germany her place in the sun, seen to be perpetrated anew. Wotan's Vandals and Goths conquered the world only to lose it to the stratagems of Rome and Byzantium. Later, impudent saints and soldiers invaded the great unconscious forests to hew down his sacred oaks. The twilight of the gods brought untimely eclipse to Valhalla. Nietzsche's pale Galilaean had conquered indeed. Wotan's very name and attributes provoke the dread of a taboo to this day.

Wotan is not just, however, the warlord of the berserkers. From his beginnings he was a shamanistic god of the underworld, versed in the wisdom of the runes, who granted to true poets the mead of inspiration. If their songs happened to be of love, then Wotan as Lord of Minne, was doubly their patron. Always it is the minstrels we must heed if we would know how it goes with soul as times change.

In Jung's view, one of the most important tasks facing modern Europe is the recognition and integration of the positive aspect of Wotan. With hindsight, Jung himself, in his life-long love affair with the anima which led him to seek wisdom amid the perils of the underworld, can now be seen as one of major manifestations of a renewed growing-point of Wotanic consciousness. The god is a psychoid reality with a special quality of energy not to be equated with that of other gods to whom he has often been likened. In his essential duplicity and his role as guide of souls he has, however, much in common with Mercury/Hermes, whose day he shares and to whom the Romans assimilated him while recognising his more warlike qualities. He is a master not only of disguises but of ambiguities, a trait well depicted by Wagner in the agonizing choice he must make between the traditional, conservative mode personified in Fricka, the goddess of marriage, and the bearer of the new consciousness, Brünnhilde. Rent by anguish, he betrays both, yet out of evil comes the end of the age of the gods and the transfer of power to humanity – a truly Aquarian dénouement.

The Valkyries who accompany him on his wild noctural hunts on the winds of winter in the ancient forests and hills of his Teutonic fief, including England, gathering the souls of the faithful departed, have affinities not with pompous Frigg/Fricka, but with her near namesake and sibylline precursor Freya, Queen of the Night and the Underworld. A twelfth-century mural in Schleswig cathedral shows her flying on a broomstick, naked but for a cloak billowing behind her, as goddess of witches. But Freya's name, unlike Wotan's, is no longer one to conjure with.

The parallel figure from the classical world, Artemis/

Diana, suffered a similar demotion under the Christian repression, becoming restricted to her Hecate role as patroness of that last persecuted remnant of the old feminine religion of nature and the earth which was stigmatized as witchcraft, though the name of Hecate herself remains a word of power and awe. But the history of the archetype and its repression date back far beyond the Christian era. Long before Wotan became a name that none might utter, the first female was expunged from the pages of Semitic mythology to become a nameless howling terror of the wilderness wreaking her vengeance on the usurping children of Adam. Yet she does have a name, no less ominous than Wotan's, against which magic and religion have been deployed throughout the millennia, a name to be conjured with today, as the proud talisman of militant feminism, Lilith. Adam's first wife who refused to submit by assuming the inferior position in love, she cursed him with the ineffable name of God, which like Isis she knew, and was banished to the depths of the Red Sea. Yet her bird, like that of personified divine wisdom, Athene, is the owl, and she herself was later described as the ladder on which the prophets ascend. In Jewish secret doctrine she becomes the bride of God, the Shekinah of the Exile.

Lilith harks back to the Age of Taurus when, as the excavations at Çatal-Hüyük indicate, women's magic was supreme and the prerogatives of the Goddess remained unchallenged. Just as the battle lust of Wotan, who rides on the storm and whose name means rage, threatens to overwhelm us unless he is redeemed, so the rage of Lilith, whose name means wind and darkness, can tear society apart if it is ignored. Blind, one-sided hatred of the male hands women over to their negative, unconscious male-ness, and, by alienating the sexes instead of encouraging them to relate, whatever the difficulties, delays the possibility of conscious androgyny. All contents emerging from long repression display first their inferior, negative aspects. Patience and sympathy are required if the base metal is to be transmuted into gold.

Beyond the Wotanic furor lies a sense of the oneness of the world and all that is in it, a trust in the reality of rebirth and a poetic, heroic intuition of the nature of the human quest, with its tragedies and ironies. Against Lilith's wish to cut up men must be set woman's rediscovery of pride in her sex – and her sexuality – irrespective of any rôle assigned to her by patriarchal society, and a new confidence, independence and objectivity which mark her out as the equal partner of man and the one who must sometimes take the lead in our common pilgrimage towards the unknown.

Chapter 2

The Astrological Pantheon

I HAVE LONG felt that when astrologers talk about planets
and psychologists talk about archetypes, both are referring
to the same relatively unknown forces that shape our lives,
the built-in patterns of behaviour through which people
express their individual humanity, or, to put it in yet
another way, the differing pre-existent channels along
which the life-force flows. I was, therefore, pleased to find
it baldly stated in a modern textbook of astrology* that
"each planet appears to represent archetypal forces functioning within man and Nature, which the ancients
personified as gods". C.G. Jung held a similar view. In a
letter to the Vice-President of the Centre International
d'Astrologie, dated 26 May 1954†, he wrote as follows:

Astrology, like the collective unconscious with which psychology is concerned, consists of symbolic configurations: the
"planets" are the gods, symbols of the powers of the unconscious . . .
What the zodiac and the planets represent are not personal traits;
they are impersonal and objective facts . . .
The interpretation of the archetypes [the gods] and their mutual
relations [is] the common concern of both arts.

At a first, somewhat literal-minded, glance, the relationship between the nine planets and such archetypes of
the collective unconscious as have been discovered is far
from obvious. In the first place, there is no generally
agreed list of archetypes to compare with the planets and

* *Astrology* by Jeff Mayo, Teach Yourself Books, London 1964
† C.G. Jung, *Letters*, Vol. 2, Routledge & Kegan Paul Plc, London 1976

probably never will be. As Jung wrote: "It is no use at all to learn a list of archetypes by heart. Archetypes are complexes of experience that come upon us like fate and their effects are felt in our most personal life."* So one would be unwise to say more about archetypes than one has experienced oneself, and everyone's experience is different. Jung's descriptions of ego, shadow, persona, anima, animus, self, trickster, puer aeternus, helpful animal, magician, hero, great mother, wise old man, etc., are based on Jung's experience and that of his patients, and are intended as aids for the differentiation and interpretation of our own experience of the psychic contents. A second difficulty is that many important and distinct European gods are not represented, or at least not overtly, among the planets.

Nevertheless, it seemed to me that, as from the psychological side at least, little had been done to follow up the leads that had been given in investigating this area of the common ground between astrology and psychology, it would be worthwhile tentatively examining the planets from the point of view of archetypal psychology, not with the intention of translating one system into another, but rather of provoking a discussion that might further mutual understanding.

The sun is, in my view, the most complex of the 'planets' from the archetypal standpoint. This is partly due to the confusion that exists between the concepts of ego and self. Astrology reflects this tension by its traditional placement of the sun as number four, the earth's position, in the order of the planets. But although it is considered as just one among the planets, it also is their source and incorporates them all within its system. Another complication concerns the mythological identity of the sun. As Helios he was undoubtedly divine but attracted relatively little cult or

* C.G. Jung, *Collected Works*, Vol. 9, pt. 1, p. 30, Routledge & Kegan Paul Plc, London 1976

folklore. Gradually, however, from the classical period onward, he became assimilated to the far from simple figure of Apollo. Professor E.R. Dodds has argued cogently in *The greeks and the Irrational** that it was primarily through the cult of Apollo, originally a mantic, shamanistic god from the North-East, possibly Scythia, whose devotees experienced prophetic trances and astral travelling, that the irrational became an important element in Greek religion. But, in the idealising world of Hellenism, Apollo's raven was eclipsed by his swan. The establishment in Europe of a monolithic empire under a deified ruler went hand in hand with the infiltration of another Eastern novelty, monotheism, centred on the solar principle. The transition from Apollo, the all-bright, shining one, to the Mithraic unconquered sun and the Christian sun of righteousness seems to have been accepted without too much difficulty throughout most of the Mediterranean world. Astrology thus became and has remained the sole bastion of the alternative, polytheistic world-view, at least until very recently.

Another apparent contradiction inherent within the sun archetype is that while it tends to become one with the dominant of consciousness, whether Apollo or Christ, and thus in due course becomes the old king, ready to be supplanted, it also signifies the youthful hero, rising as the potential supplanter at the winter solstice or in the cusp of the Platonic great years. Eternally, John the Baptist, he of the summer solstice, must set so that the divine child of Christmas shall rise. And what new avatar will the dawning of the age of Aquarius bring forth? In the waiting time we need to be aware both of how one-sided our Apollonian old king has become and of what unlived potentiality yet remains within him. The dominant of consciousness for us has come full cycle from his irrational origins, to represent an ultra-rational, objective, intellec-

* Beacon Paperbacks, Boston, 1957

tual attitude. What has suffered has been all that is represented by his split-off dark brother, Dionysus, the tortuous, muddy path in the forest, ecstatic, uncontrolled, libidinous. Perhaps we need to recall that Apollo, the pure and spiritual, was once, too, a rustic god of flocks and herds, a god of magic, possession and inspiration, father of healing and sender of pestilence, whose sacred animals include the wolf, the stag, the snake, the mouse, the cock and the dolphin; lord, through the muses, of dance, song, gaiety and erotic poetry. No less should we forget Jesus the shepherd, the carpenter, vine and bringer of wine, the Lord of the Dance, who rescued and raised up the fallen feminine principle.

I shall summarise how I see in psychological terms the archetype of the sun. These terms are the ego-self axis, and the transformations in the relationship between self and ego in the course of the individuation process. The self is psychic totality, the original, unconscious, all-inclusive, genetic potentia, from which, at first in isolated flashes in early childhood, the ego, subject of consciousness, emerges. The ego on its hero-path of achievement, slaying the dragon of dependence on mother and family, taking responsibility for being an individual in a world of individuals, one-sidedly plays its strong suits and journeys ever further from its first home, ascribing everything to its own strength and cleverness. At some point, however, the fascinating pull of the primal wholeness reasserts itself and, from the subsequent agony of awakening, death and rebirth, a new alignment is constellated. The relativised ego acknowledges the existence of the other psychic contents and becomes aware of its responsibility as the exponent of the self, its source and its goal, as well as the path between, and the urge to tread it. "I am alpha and omega, the way, the truth and the life." Jesus, the individuating ego, is baptized into the divine archon, Christ, and the great work begins, as always, with temptation in the wilderness. Later, perhaps, under the shadow of the opposite-reconciling cross, in the holding of the tension between being a child of earth and of starry heaven it may also be said, "I and the Father are one". Thus Jung, in the great book of his old age, *Mysterium Coniunctionis*, almost teasingly uses the terms 'ego' and 'self' as if they were interchangeable.

All the other planets symbolize different aspects of the solar journey of individuation, archetypal situations and modes of being that the soul needs to experience in its quest for wholeness. Energy flows forth from the sun to the uttermost planet and back again; the circulatory systems in their circumambulation of the body and all its members pass through the glandular orbits in their journey of regeneration and self-regulation to keep the whole and its parts in harmony and balance.

The first and irreducible balancing act is that between Yang and Yin and brings us at once face to face with the inadequacies of language, for men are not always active nor women passive, as might be inferred from the way in which we talk about the masculine and feminine principles. In other myths and languages the sun is feminine and the moon a god. So when I say feminine, I do not mean female or solely pertaining to women, but a mode of being common to both sexes. Thus, although we may be somewhat short of planetary goddesses, it seems likely, following this principle, that each planet has, so to speak, a masculine and a feminine pole. We are helped also by the fact that the moon herself is a triple goddess, mirroring in her phases different archetypal enactments of the feminine principle.

There is yet another difficulty which we have experienced already, though not referred to, in connection with Apollo, and which becomes particularly acute when it is goddesses that we are considering. This is the phenomenon which I shall call archetypal shift, that is the process whereby, when an observer considers the pantheon as a group, or even each archetype in isolation, individual distinctions become blurred and everything becomes equal to everything else in a grand Olympian salad. This is because they are all aspects of total reality and reflect that totality. We are all part of the *unus mundus*, but astrology and psychology, as compasses for use on the dark journey to that realisation, are concerned with delineating and differentiating the various landmarks, sometimes, it may seem, exaggeratedly and artificially. This analysis, splitting-off, dissolving into prime elements, is in fact an indispensable preliminary to reintegration. The trouble with goddesses is that they all tend to turn into the great mother archetype from which they derive, just as men tend, however unlikely and unpromising the material, to turn all women into their mothers. Mythologically there is an extensive repertoire of feminine archetypal possibilities but, historically, the practical possibilities for most women in everyday life have been strictly limited, and the way we look at the planets reflects these limitations.

Key-words associated with the moon in astrology are: instinct, habit, heredity, mother, feeling, memory, imagination, receptivity, impressionability, fluctuation, fluidity and mediation. Mythologically, the original Greek moon-goddess, Selene, had little cult, though in Hellenistic times she was believed to be the abode of souls, an idea given new currency in the teachings of the Gurdjieff school, which also subscribes to the Endymion myth that sees the moon as a cosmic hypnotist keeping mankind in a state of sleep. Apart from Selene, the goddesses with whom the moon has been chiefly associated are Artemis (or Diana), Hera and Hecate within the Graeco-Roman tradition, though many of these attributes were to be subsumed in the cult of Isis and, later still, in the hyperdulia accorded to the Blessed Virgin Mary.

The first phase of the moon belongs to Artemis the maid, the virgin of the Annunciation, belonging to no man, at one with herself and one-in-herself, (running wild in the forests with the animals), huntress rather than quarry, woman as a piece of untamed nature. When the moon is full, Selene assumes her Hera role of adult, wife and mother, the nourishing cow, but also "la vache enragée", the gravity pull of collectivity and the guardian of custom, secretary-general of the wives' and mothers' trades union. The third phase is that of the waning and the dark moon, the domain of Hecate, the black virgin and the pietà, the witch, the crone and – to men at least – the dark, terrifying and devouring aspect of women's mysteries.

Archetypally the moon represents, I suggest, the feminine principle in its undifferentiated form as the organic and rhythmical process within nature, encompassing fertility, growth and decay, coming to be and passing away, the Way of Seeming in the dichotomy of Parmenides, the veil of Maya masking the reality behind appearances and endlessly seducing mankind into taking them for the whole truth so that the purposes of nature shall be blindly served.

To the masculine principle in its hero mode the moon is "that old serpent that deceives the world", the eternally superior wisdom of the feminine that knows all the works of men are vain and ephemeral, a boy's boast of "I'm the king of the castle" while already the tide laps round the sandy foundations – in short, the mother complex, a deadly dragon whether it comes forth through its positive or negative portal. But for those who have awakened from its spell, it is the guardian and bestower of great treasure, for it is the left eye of God, a mitigated form of consciousness that does not scorch or desiccate but reveals the figures of the imaginal realm in dreams and visions and allows them to be themselves as natural phenomena. It is the feminine wisdom that allows things to happen rather than busily organizing them into preconceived forms. Thus she becomes not the prison of souls but the gate of heaven. Innocent III, the Pope of St. Francis and St.

Dominic, wrote of her: "Towards the Moon it is he should look, who is buried in the shades of sin and iniquity. Having lost grace, the day disappears and there is no more sun for him, but the Moon is still on the horizon. Let him address himself to Mary; under her influence thousands every day find their way to God."

The third member of the primal trinity and partaking of the nature of both sun and moon is Mercury, of whom the alchemists said: "Mercurius duplex, utriusque capax", double and capable of either. Like Apollo, Mercury, a highly complex god, has become simplified and special- ised by the erosion of the centuries, from which not even astrology is immune. Hermes appears first as a gentle death-god or the god of a gentle death, a summoner of souls to undertake the journey out of incarnation. Thus he becomes the guide of souls and messenger of the gods. He is also from earliest times the ithyphallic herm symboliz- ing fertility and immortality, the potency of life and death, father, according to some versions, of Pan, Eros and Priapus, carrier of the ram and Dionysus. His is a nonheroic mode depending for success on intelligence and cunning, so that Odysseus is naturally his protégé and ideal exponent, but for all to whom life is an adventure he is the psychopomp. He is both old and young, male and female, inventor of language and lover of nymphs. His is the grace which builds on nature, the divine harmony of the spiritual and the animal. He is a shameless, mocking, roguish, thieving trickster, god of traders and entre- preneurs as well as of secret love affairs and the music of love, ruler of dreams and coincidences, lord of meeting and finding, gain and loss. Through him we become conscious by remembering ourselves, our origin and our reason for being. His science of hermeneutics teaches divine secrets about the meaning revealed in appearances. He is the principle of transformation and evolution, god in nature, and unity in duality, the beginning, middle and end of the work, the *lapis* and the process, the *prima materia* and the goal of his own transformation. In astrology, in his highest aspect, Mercury is the planet of the adept, just as he is, I suspect, in the Tarot, both "Le Mat" and "Le Bateleur". In all this he has a subtly complementary relation to Saturn, as puer to senex.

It is one of the chief qualities of the volatile spirit Mercurius that he will not be pinned down, nor submit to being put in a bottle and labelled. How then to try and do him justice in psychological terms? He is clearly more than the superficial clever Dick, the talented secondary school teacher of the horoscope that popular astrology has tended to make of him. Could we perhaps say of Mercury that he is for depth psychology the archetypal representation of that hard to grasp principle which Jung calls the transcendent function, a process which facilitates a transition from one attitude to another? He writes of it in *Psychological Types** as follows: "The raw material shaped by thesis and antithesis, and in the shaping of which the opposites are united, is the living symbol. Its profundity of meaning is inherent in the raw material itself, the very stuff of the psyche, transcending time and dissolution; and its configuration by the opposites ensures its sovereign power over all the psychic functions."

If the archetype of the moon stands for the rhythmic, cyclical, natural processes of fertilisation, growth, decay and regeneration, the undifferentiated Yin principle, Venus represents the dynamic force of attraction between Yin and Yang, that element in the eternal feminine that leads us on – and into life. Jung called the anima "the archetype of life" and in old age wrote of the active feminine in striking terms:

Being that has soul is living being. Soul is the living thing in man, and that which lives of itself and causes life. Therefore God

* *C.W.* Vol. 6, p. 480

breathed into Adam a living breath, that he might live. With her cunning play of illusions the soul lures into life the inertness of matter that does not want to live. She makes us believe incredible things that life may be lived. She is full of snares and traps in order that man should fall, should reach the earth, entangle himself there, and stay caught, so that life should be lived; as Eve in the garden of Eden could not rest content until she had convinced Adam of the goodness of the forbidden apple. Were it not for the leaping and twinkling of the soul, man would rot away in his greatest passion, idleness.*

Venus is not all roses and violets, doves and sparrows. The tiger, too, is a Yin animal, and it was the apprehension of the goddess in such a dreadful aspect that inspired the awe-struck outcry in Racine's *Phèdre*:

"C'est Vénus toute entière, à sa proie attachée!"

Geoffrey Grigson in *The Goddess of Love*[†] shows how Venus has been idealised and bowdlerised throughout the Christian era, especially by classical scholars.

I suspect that this process may even have affected astrology, which, while it gives due weight to the earthy aspects of the planetary influence, has also, by enthroning her as one of the benefics, tended to obscure the principle that all archetypes possess a negative and a positive pole. But the greatest injustice perpetrated against her has been at the hands of spiritualisers of all denominations, who, while acknowledging her as goddess of love, give a thoroughly one-sided interpretation to that much abused word. For Aphrodite is the goddess of lechery as well as tenderness. Born from the foam stirred up by the wriggling genitals of Uranus, lopped off into the Aegean, she is herself a lover of genitals, Aphrodite Philommedes. As Porné she is the whore and patroness of whores and brothels. One of the main features of her cult was sacred prostitution, not only in Cyprus and Asia Minor but on the mainland of Greece and in Italy. All sexual desire,

*C.W. Vol. 1, p. 26f.

[†] Constable, 1976

whatever the object desired, belongs to her as Queen of the Orgasm. She is the mother of Priapus and Eros; the goat is her sacrificial animal and other fauna and flora associated with her mostly have sexual connotations. She is also a lover of laughter and postponer of old age; the love that finds a way and laughs at locksmiths, Peitho, the persuader. To the Greeks she was not the planet itself but evening and morning star belonged to her because they marked the time for lovers to come and to depart.

Many of her attributes were taken over by the new Queen of Heaven, Mary, including, thanks to the error of a scribe in copying 'stella maris' instead of 'stilla' from a text of Jerome, the guardianship of sailors. The lily, the rose and springs of water as well as the colour blue belong naturally to both, and both, despite the idealisation process, are sometimes represented as black. According to one myth, Aphrodite is child of earth and sky and, by her own attributes, links them together. Mary's function is similar as mediatrix, carrier of prayers from earth to heaven, bestower of graces from heaven to earth. This may be a pointer to the way in which we should consider Venus as archetype: that power behind love and sex which we might without fear of idealisation call the principle of relatedness, or, after her son, the Eros principle.

Mars is, at first sight, as befits a blunt warrior, the most straightforward of the planets. Prominent in Rome, he was to the Greeks, as Ares, an unpopular deity, with little cult, curiously unheroic for a god of war, even, at times, ridiculous. He is ignominiously driven off in single combat with his lame brother Hephaestus who, on another occasion, traps him *in flagrante delicto* with Aphrodite by means of a magic net and exhibits him to the rest of Olympus. In yet another humiliation he is knocked out by Athene. Astrology links him with the gonads, the muscles and the adrenals, the glands of fight and flight. His key-words are: passion, courage, desire, energy, assertiveness, initiative, anger, blood, fire, iron, impatience and aggression. If Venus is a more specifically physical and personal manifestation of the generalised, lunar, feminine principle, Mars plays a similar role vis-à-vis the sun. His chief animal symbol is the wild boar with its furious charge and its thick skin. For man he is the blind, unconscious outflow of libido whether it takes the direction of ambition and the power-drive, explodes in autonomous affect or fuels the ruthless thrust of the unrelated male sexual shadow. As far as his role in feminine psychology is concerned, it is worth noting that he is very much the son of his mother Hera, little attention being paid to the question of his paternity, and that wild boars tend to be the instrument of the Great Mother to destroy the son-lover. Thus we could see him too as the battling, invincible, insensitive, castrating animus in general and, in particular, the dangers to the youthful hero of the destructive mother animus. When the energy of Mars does not flow in its appropriate channels, which are the instinct of self-preservation and, when yoked with Venus, the sex drive, it is indeed the troublesome malefic which traditional astrology depicts.

The key concept connected with Jupiter is expansion, and since this has generally been regarded throughout history as a good thing, it is not surprising that attention has been focused on the positive qualities of what is called the greater benefic. It is only in recent years that anyone seriously questioned the advantages of ever-increasing economic growth or that nations took measures to reduce their own populations. One of the negative consequences of expansion that has led to the widespread adoption of the slogan "small is beautiful" throughout the developed world is inflation, a word strongly associated, in my view, with the archetypal Jupiter. There is a Greek term 'até' which means infatuation or delusion and is often personified as the author of all blind, rash actions and their results.

There are a number of gods who may inflict on a mortal the punishment of até, but from the time of Homer this divine madness is above all associated with Zeus, and is sometimes called his eldest daughter. It is a fey mood of over-weening, over-confident self-destructiveness that always seems to accompany identification with an archetype. In depth psychology it is viewed, almost with horror, as one of the most dangerous psychic states, and is given the name of inflation. Such is the negative aspect of Jupiter. In general terms he seems to me to represent that archetypal voice of God which tells mankind to be fruitful and multiply and grow in wisdom and stature in accord with the principle of divine justice that is the real conscience belonging to the higher mind. Without the optimism of Jupiter, man would lack the ability to follow his urges and impulses into the adventures and experiences which alone can lead him to greater consciousness. To condense into one psychological term the archetype that Jupiter embodies, it is the principle of extraversion.

In the cosmic and microcosmic dance of the opposites, extraversion evokes its partner, introversion, and who shall say that one is better than the other? So Jupiter might spill over and flood the world were there no divine force of containment, restriction and limitation. This is the realm of Saturn, the ring-pass-not, who purifies man of the dross of unreality, through suffering. His is the lead of melancholy and despair, but he also is king of the Age of Gold. As Satan, son and left hand of God, he imposes tribulations that force man into the way of involution and introversion and gives him the perseverance and self-discipline to follow it to its conclusion. In *Saturn; a new look at an old devil**, Liz Greene has shown that Saturn is far from being just the gloomy greater malefic of popular belief but "a symbol of the psychic process, natural to all

* Samuel Weiser, New York 1976

human beings, by which an individual may utilise the experiences of pain, restriction and discipline as a means for greater consciousness and fulfilment . . . it is through him alone that we may achieve eventual freedom and self-understanding."* Dr. Niel Micklem writes from the psychological side of the bridge in strikingly similar terms in the 1975 issue of *Harvest*: "At the lowest house in astrology and the starting point of lead in the alchemists' great work, Saturn is the 'Principium Individuationis'. Depression is more than illness. It is an archetypal manifestation of psychic necessity. It is individuation."

Of the extra-Saturnian planets in general my feeling is that, while they have in a remarkable way acquired the names of gods which appropriately denote the influences they represent, they also radiate other qualities or archetypal modes which are re-emerging after a long repression or are, perhaps, new contents now reaching human consciousness for the first time. Thus, in considering these planets, we should also have in mind the archetypal forms which have suffered the greatest degree of eclipse and repression during the Christian era. These are, I believe, Dionysus, Pan and, to step out of the classical world for a moment, Wotan. On the other hand we should be attentive to whatever new vibrations may now be reaching us through the ether from the Age of Aquarius.

It is still a matter of debate among astrologers as to whether the extra-Saturnian planets should be accorded the rulership of any zodiacal sign. The entry of these planets into new signs *in caelo* is, however, an indisputable fact of great interest for augurs who observe the Zeitgeist. Since 1914 each entry of Pluto, for example, into a new constellation, has not on the whole coincided with periods of peace and stability. Will the present transition of the Lord of the Underworld into Scorpio portend increased

*pp. 10 et seq.

crime, subversion, terrorism and cruelty, or will the qualities of the planet dignified by its presence in a sign so congenial to it, help to foster a more creative relationship to the deep unconscious? Neptune's entry into Capricorn in 1984 could be expected to synchronize with the latter development by the dissolution of barriers and rigid attitudes belonging to the past.

The characteristics of Uranus are less related to the mythological background than is the case with Neptune and Pluto. This is partly because Uranus, like sky-gods throughout the world, tends to become a remote 'deus otiosus', without much cult or mythic material, the fertilising consort of Mother Earth, far off in the dream time. Also a certain logic dictates that as, in the order of planets, the one after Jupiter is his father and predecessor Saturn, so the next planet to be discovered should be named for Saturn's sire. Nevertheless, the sky is the source of unexpected and mysterious events such as electric storms, lightning, fire-balls, supernovae, comets, hail-storms and rushing, mighty winds and such phenomena are fully in accord with the astrological description of Uranus. Key words belonging to the Uranian life-principle include: drastic change, revolution, independence, inspiration, deviance and inventiveness. It was discovered at the beginning of the Industrial Revolution, between the American and French Revolutions and at the dawn of the ·Romantic Revival. The physical planet Uranus is the eccentric individualist of the Solar System, having an extraordinary axial inclination of more than ninety degrees. One result of this is that each pole has successively a night lasting 21 terrestrial years. One of the principles on which the *I Ching* is based is the tendency for something to turn into its opposite. Jung used the richly resonant term of Heraclitus to denote this tendency – 'enantiodromia', a running contrary ways, or between the opposites. Thus the sudden, though long gestated, overthrow of tyranny in the name of freedom and independence leads through chaos to another sudden revolution and the establishment of a yet more oppressive tyranny. In the psyche, after long work in the dark, an entirely new attitude may suddenly flash like lightning and show everything in a different light, but even that new attitude will one day crystallise into an old restrictive norm, hindering the individual's need for full self-expression until it, too, has to be transcended and superseded. Such is the renewing role of Uranus in the unconscious.

Although Neptune was actually sighted in 1795, it was not discovered as a planet until 1846. In that year, ether was introduced into surgical practice and C.G. Carus published his work *Psyche* with its Romantic approach to the unconscious. Braid had just coined the term 'hypnotism' to denote the new technique of artificially inducing, by suggestion, a state resembling deep sleep. Mediumistic spiritualism as a popular phenomenon can be said to have originated in 1848 when Mrs. Fox invited her neighbours to witness the strange rapping noises that occurred whenever her two daughters were present. The same year saw the publication of the Communist Manifesto, idealistic revolutions all over Europe and the departure of emigrants in great waves to seek a better life over the sea. Photography, cigarettes, mass entertainments for the vast new urban populations, a taste for the bizarre and occult in literature and a proliferation of new, idealistic, religious sects all belong to this period.

The sense of vagueness, boundlessness, illusoriness that diffuses from all this accords well enough with mythological Poseidon, god of the sea and father of its mythical denizens, and the Roman Neptune who rules all waters. I view the planet archetypally as symbolizing both the intuitive function and the imaginal realm which it can explore and inhabit by means of creative fantasy. Blake's phrase "Jesus the imagination" and his conception of imagination as "the real and eternal world of which the Vegetable Universe is but a faint shadow" is suggestive to me of the true significance of the Neptunian archetype.

The discovery of Pluto coincided with the Depression and the ensuing New Deal, the era of the great dictators and the mid-point between the two world wars. The secrets underlying the world of appearances were being increasingly probed and revealed by astronomy, nuclear physics, archaeology, economics and depth psychology, which entered into its hey-day at this time. A cult of violence, death and nihilism was the order of the day: in Germany, Wotan re-emerged in his most negative aspect; the underworld of organised crime terrorised America; the atomic bomb became a possibility; Spain destroyed itself to the cry of "Viva la Muerte"; and Freud defined and refined the principle of Thanatos, the archetypal death-wish. The iconoclastic Existentialism of Sartre stems from this period as well as the sexually releasing work of Gide, D.H. Lawrence and Henry Miller.

Mythologically, Pluto is the ruler of the underworld and the dead, the darkest brother of Zeus, Hades, the Unseen, the Rich One, the Rapist of Persephone. In astrology, the idea chiefly connected with Pluto is transformation and renewal through elimination. He has been assigned the rulership of Scorpio with its emphasis on the sexual symbolism of death and rebirth. One recalls the subterranean *mysterium coniunctionis* performed at Eleusis, after which the initiate no longer feared death. A revival of the ancient mysteries in a form appropriate to the day is also one of the signs of the times associated with the discovery of Pluto, and may well represent his essential archetypal significance. Many gurus and masters have appeared in the West over the past half century to tell in their own ways of the mystery of death and rebirth as a psychological reality, but it is, in my belief, more in accord with the meaning of the new planets, considered in their totality as three wise men attending the birth of the Aquarian aeon, that man today must make his own individual descent into the depths and find his interior teacher. I propose, therefore, to leave the last word to Jung, whose conviction this was, from a letter in which he renounced the idea of being a guru.

I don't want to addle anybody's brains with my subjective conjectures . . . I have had experiences [but] . . . the prejudices aroused by their telling might block other people's way to a living and wondrous mystery . . . so I don't want to seduce anyone into believing and thus take his experience from him . . . But one thing I will tell you: the exploration of the unconscious has in fact and in truth discovered the age-old timeless way of initiation . . . Nothing is submerged for ever – that is the terrifying discovery everyone makes who has opened that portal . . . Now it is not merely my credo but the greatest and most incisive experience in my life that this door, a highly inconspicuous side-door on an unsuspicious-looking and easily overlooked footpath – narrow and indistinct because only a few have set foot on it – leads to the secret of transformation and renewal.*

---

* Letter to Professor B. Baur-Celio, 30th January 1934, C.G. Jung, *Letters*, Vol. 1, Routledge and Kegan Paul Plc, London 1973

Chapter 3

The World: Proving Ground of the Soul

LITURGY, THE form of public worship, has always been considered one of the most anthropologically significant statements that a society makes about itself. In the days when the services of the Church of England were still regulated according to the Book of Common Prayer, there were periodically things called Rogation Days, which included the chanting of the Litany. In magnificent, thunderous English, we would ask to be preserved from pride, vainglory, hypocrisy, envy, hatred, malice and fornication – clearly sins which were our responsibility and, God willing, subject to our control. Then, on the other hand, there were events more under the rubric of what insurance companies call acts of God: "Lightning, tempest, plague, pestilence, famine, battle, murder, sudden death, sedition, privy conspiracy, rebellion" – matters beyond our control that simply befell us. In one supplication however, a different order of evils is mentioned, not exactly either sins or afflictions, but *a priori* conditions of our being. "From all the deceits of the World, the Flesh and the Devil, Good Lord, deliver us." What is the status of these entities? Are they inside or outside or both? I suggest that they should be approached as archetypes which manifest as autonomous psychoid forces in that middle realm where what we call spirit and matter interact.

However tempting it may be to follow the flesh and the devil, it is primarily with the world that I shall be dealing here. I shall consider the twentieth-century individual in relation to the world from two and ultimately three points of view. The first of these is the outer world, the world of appearances. We sometimes beg the biggest question in philosophy by calling this the real world. Parmenides of Elea, who was born in the sixth century BC, wrote a philosophical poem about the Way of Seeming and the Way of Truth, in which he argues that the multitude of sense objects which come into existence and then pass away in time, cannot be considered as true Being, which is motionless and changeless. Much of subequent philosophy has been an attempt to resolve the problem posed by Parmenides – the problem of saving the appearances.

Jesus Christ, who proclaimed himself the Way and the Truth, pointed to the potentially perilous nature of this world he came to save, for one who would save his soul. "For what shall it profit a man, if he gain the whole world and lose his own soul?" "Be of good cheer, I have overcome the world." The devil, that old deceiver, is the Prince of this world, the world of appearances which Hinduism defines even more explicitly as Maya – Illusion. In psychological terms, why is this world such a peril to the soul? The world is, after all, also other people, and man, being a gregarious animal, cannot individuate in a vacuum.

The growth of consciousness and a sense of I go hand in hand with the development of speech and reason which derive in turn from interaction with the world of objects, appearances and fellow human beings. But the originality and individuality of expression that are such a delightful feature of early childhood are soon blighted by the pressures to adapt and conform to the expectations of other people. The ego is in the process of formation when a child begins to differentiate itself from others and say "I". But when it ceases to find in the environment the right nourishment for its own essential nature, and succumbs to the temptation to appear in the way other people require it to be, it begins to form a mask, or persona, and to cut itself off from the source of being. The persona, according to Jung: "is nothing real . . . it is a compromise between an individual and society as to what a man should appear to be. The less it is based on the constitutional reality of the individual, the more it will be a 'mask of the collective psyche', hiding one's true nature from oneself as well as from others".*

Jung acknowledged the necessity for a flexible persona based on the individual's physical and psychological constitution, his ego-ideal and the collective ideal of the period. In most of his writings, however, he treats the persona as, at best, a necessary evil, and at worst, something very close to what the existentialist Heidegger defines as fallen being, or inauthenticity. Fallen being is characterised by what Heidegger calls temptation, apparent tranquillity and alienation from self. The temptation is to follow the line of least resistance by identifying with the collective, masking one's flight from self by chatter, inquisitiveness and ambiguity. Chatter is talk which is less concerned with the topic under discussion than with what others say about it. Inquisitiveness is the search for novelty, not to increase one's understanding, but as a Pascalian "divertissement" to save us from having to face our own reality or lack of it. We gain in return the illusion of having interesting, intellectually active lives, always up to the minute with the latest trend. Through inquisitiveness the inauthentic man falls into a state of ambiguity in which he no longer knows what he really knows and what he doesn't know, but seems to know everything since he is interested in everything and talks about everything.

The second characteristic of the state of fallenness is tranquillity. Reassured by the opinion of others, one lives at peace, feeling adapted to one's milieu and adopting all its ideas. Finally, the fallen being experiences alienation

* *C.W.* Vol. 7, Routledge & Kegan Paul Plc (1953)

from self, through conformity with the world. One has ceased to be oneself, lost in the universality of collective man.

In Gurdjieff's system, too, the true nature with which we are born, essence, is gradually and inevitably overlaid by layers of personality deriving from the influence of others. A further and negative stage of development is the growth of what he calls false personality, that is, the tendency to ascribe one's borrowed plumes to oneself, feeling special and proud and individual about the second-hand acquisitions, thus cutting oneself off from essence, which may have remained stuck at the age of three or four.

Both Jung and Gurdjieff stress the importance of developing a strong ego or rich personality for the purposes of individuation, or the Work. For Gurdjieff, the rich personality can become passive at a certain stage, while essence becomes active and is nourished by personality as the germ feeds on the yolk in an egg. For Jung, only a strong ego can withstand the encounter with the other contents of the psyche and come to sense itself as the exponent of the unknown subject, or supraordinate principle, acting within the psyche, that he called the self. Both of them saw the identification with the persona, or false personality (though those two concepts are not identical), and the tendency to identify with it, as a major obstacle to be overcome in the search for reality.

It is not my particular concern here to draw parallels between the teachings of Jung, Gurdjieff and Heidegger – the ideas of one system can never be adequately translated into those of another – but rather to show how those very different twentieth-century men of ideas, wielding considerable influence in their own divergent fields of psychology, esotericism and philosophy, shared, though all would have denied it, a wide measure of agreement in their view of the interaction of the individual and the collective in the individuation process.

The world as collective consciousness, and the world of

the collective unconscious, intersect at the point where an individual identifies with an archetype whether directly or, via projection, on to another person, an idea or a cause. The sort of examples of this usually given are Hitler's Nuremberg rallies, a football crowd and the adulation accorded to pop stars, but there are less dramatic instances to hand which affect us all at some point in our lives. Some experience of it may indeed be a necessary part of the individuation process. Joseph Henderson postulated three conditions for individuation*:

1 separation from the original family or clan,
2 commitment to a meaningful group, over a long period of time and
3 liberation from too close an identity with the group.

As the family or clan has become weakened, so the need to belong, to experience the sense of security that comes from we-consciousness and togetherness, has become ever more pressing. Relationship or community is seen as the god that will save us, and inevitably it crumbles under the weight of such expectation. The contemporary view of marriage, for example, presupposes the desirability of a far greater amount of time spent together by the couple than was the case a generation ago, or in tribal societies which practise a considerable degree of segregation. It is for example commonly expected nowadays that a couple should *want* to do everything together – the ultimate triumph of Wendy's philosophy over Peter Pan's.

The decline of traditional religion, disillusionment with political panaceas and an apparent lack of new fields for the pioneering spirit to explore have increasingly led people to seek the meaning of their lives in relationships. Eros, as relatedness, is, some say, the oldest and the greatest of the gods, but like any god viewed in a one-sided, literalistic way and asked the wrong questions, he tends to turn

* *Thresholds of Initiation* by Joseph L. Henderson, p. 197, Wesleyan University Press, (1967)

tricksterish and negative. Marriage, for example, is not his domain but Hera's and today, more than ever, her traditional model seems inadequate to fulfil all the requirements placed on the erotic ideal. Serial monogamy, until age reduces expectations, seems not to be the solution, merely providing the opportunity of repeating neurotic patterns of behaviour with a variety of partners, to be changed whenever encounter with the shadow and one's personal difficulties become too painful. No other arrangement, such as open multiple relationships, living together without marriage or solitary existence with occasional forays, offers in itself any greater hope of providing the material of self-fulfilment unless accompanied by a radical change of attitude. Such an attitude would have to include a willingness to learn from the other about the nature of the contrasexual element potential in oneself.

Women need to learn to be able to see things less personally; to experience the pleasures of objectivity; live more in the here and now. Men need to learn to value relationship for its own sake; become more of a whole, less compartmentalized. Above all a bridge of understanding must be built across the chasm of divergent genetic programming which impels man to go out and fertilize as many women as possible so that his all-conquering genes may march down the generations, and woman, with her limited supply of precious eggs, to safeguard her posterity by choosing with great care the one who is to fertilize her, subsequently holding on to him in the face of all rivals as long as she and her offspring need security and protection.

Individuation does not take place in a vacuum, and even in Tantric Yoga a tangible partner of the opposite sex is a necessary prerequisite to embarking on a relationship with one's own shakti. The journey towards self-realisation lies on the path of unitive knowledge and conjunction with the inner soul-mate who is our fate. But the first part of that journey presupposes that we are firmly based on the mode that belongs to our own sex. Failing this, the desired androgyny will be unconscious and of little value for individual evolution.

Before the master-work with the animus/anima, the individual will already have needed tb discover something of his identity through interaction with the collective and discovery of the shadow. To make up for their loss of roots our urban nomads in the West have tended to merge their existence with that of the group, whether political, religious or recreational, but the energy available for transformation is low and crude. St. Paul on the road to Damascus was already totally committed with all his being to one set of convictions and was converted from one mighty myth to one of even higher mana. To switch one's support from Celtic to Rangers would indeed be a radical transformation with religious and tribal undertones, but the energy of a big archetypal idea powerful enough to transform a whole personality would be lacking in a declining culture. As the trivial becomes important and the important is trivialized, everything becomes the same temperature and subsides towards a state of Laodicean entropy, which is displeasing to the gods. "Because thou art neither hot nor cold, I will spew thee out of my mouth."* Energizing transformations occur only between collective faiths which still have energy, and today in the West that means mainly Communism and Christianity. Solzhenitzyn's baptism of fire transformed him into a Christian spokesman whose authority, whether we agree with him or not, is undeniable. His conversion is wholly serious and individual, though the Christian myth is a collective one.

Heidegger's inauthentic being on the other hand is entropically at one with the received ideas of the day that act as a kind of neutral, psychological wallpaper to the life of the herd, mental clichés which are taken for granted as

---

* *The Book of Revelation*, 3, xv

self-evident truths that need not be questioned or even noticed. There was, for example, a whole package of vague ideas and unexamined assumptions current and fashionable until recently, that represented the conventional wisdom of the so-called liberal establishment, to which it was expected that educated and informed people should subscribe.

The commitment to a meaningful group, however, and, almost inevitably, some identification with its aims and ethos, is very much more potent. Eyes sparkle, voices ring with conviction, while humour, objectivity and the critical faculty fly out of the window. Very often there is projection of the self on to some charismatic leader or idealistic system, and projection of the shadow on to enemies real or imagined, or on to the uninitiated. An autonomous feeling-toned complex, rich in associations, is formed round an archetypal core, and is activated whenever one is with the group, or if any association to the group or its ideas arises. When one talks to someone possessed by such a complex, it is like coming up against a hard intractable road-block in the mind, an uncompromising sub-personality that can easily turn fanatical and ruthless. Infallible within his closed system of ideas and values, or his adulation of the god-like teacher, the disciple, unaware that he is under a spell, generates an amazing amount of energy thanks to the spurious single-pointedness and purity of heart that he is experiencing. All contradictions seem capable of solution in the blinding clarity of the truth that he sees, and the possessed one feels full of meaning and life.

Such an experience can supplant received ideas and old collective religious beliefs and myths, leading the individual onto his or her own path. Usually, however, the individual follows a safer way already trodden by the many and acceptable to society. At the worst, the individual is induced to report what has been experienced to a psychiatrist, to be returned to normality by means of drugs or other physical treatment.

I am not, incidentally, suggesting that all experiences of groups are harmful to the individual, but one needs to develop a certain inner taste in relation to one's experience. There is, for example, the feeling of joy and love that sometimes comes as a result of a group experience, a feeling that is not related to any particular person, idea or aim, that is humbling rather than inflating, and comes like a grace to transcend one's usual sense of oneself.

The Age of Aquarius which is now upon us is sometimes said to be the age of groups, as well as the age in which the individual may have the opportunity to grow up into his own priest and king. In spite of the benefit which some may have experienced for their own individuation from working with groups, one has to say that getting stuck in a group is stunting and stultifying to an individual. On all sides we see the individual burdened by collective pressures to conform.

The rigidity that results from this process, limiting the individual's capacity for self-discovery, is part of the Saturnian quality within Aquarius, cramping the Uranian potentiality for creative self-expression. During the transition to the new age, modern myths reveal the process that is taking place. No longer affrighted by the eternal silence of infinite space, astronauts, in fact and fiction, brave the mysteries of the cosmos and the depths of their own psyche. Some come through the initiation more truly themselves from having learnt to use the force that is with them. In an ambiguous world in which right and wrong are no longer clearly defined by external authority, the evolution of consciousness depends on the individual's personal integrity, free from the need to identify with collective causes or ideals.

Everywhere, people in the grip of their own power complex and blinded by the fascinating vision of some hypothetical general good in the future, have succeeded in imposing their will on their fellow men. "The best lack all conviction while the worst are full of a passionate intensity." Yeats's words well describe the malady of the world today.

Jung said "Resistance to the organised mass can be effected only by the one who is as well organised in his individuality as the mass itself."* The question arises "How is it possible to become thus well organised in one's individuality?"

The answer lies, I believe, not in the strength of ego, but in the strength of the ego's link with the transcendental source. Many who have triumphed over the crushing oppression of Communism and National Socialism are people who have found their own living link to the God of their tradition. Perhaps, if we were under Soviet domination, we should turn again to the God of our fathers, but as it is, for many of us, the Church is no longer a vessel of individual salvation but one more public transport vehicle leading to a rather collective-looking destination. More and more people today are looking within to their own experience for the way of individuation, which Jung described and demonstrated.

Individuation implies not only opposition to collective norms, for that could be the mere crankiness or eccentricity of an ego unaware of the self and of the law of its own true nature. Indeed, it demands a degree of adaptation to the world of outer reality, though it cannot be found there. It can certainly not be achieved by the imitation of Jung or some other admired figure.

The inward part of the journey consists of the ego's encounter with the other contents of the psyche, of whose existence it is, to begin with, quite unconscious. During the early period of ego formation in childhood, much that is unacceptable to authority figures becomes repressed into the unconscious, or lingers in semi-awareness as an aspect of oneself which seems both inferior and shameful. Later

* *The Undiscovered Self,* vide supra p. 60, or *C.W.,* Vol. 10, p. 278

in life these contents are often projected on to others who then appear as hated enemies or despised inferiors. The first stage that usually occurs in the interior part of the individuation process – that is to say, after the ego has formed itself through adaptation to, and later, differentiation from, the collective environment – is the acknowledgement of the shadow and the struggle to integrate as part of one's own nature the repressed or projected material. Also, during the early years, reinforcement is generally given to those aspects of the personality which fit in with the sexual stereotypes of the day. As a result, the contrasexual elements, though not necessarily in themselves considered inferior, merely inappropriate, are correspondingly repressed into unconsciousness. Little girls don't play football, little boys don't play with dolls.

Neither the shadow nor the anima/animus consist solely of contents repressed into the personal layer of the unconscious, but, as archetypes, they have their roots in the *collective* unconscious, and have both positive and negative poles. To the extent that these disturbing psychic components are projected on to other people, they are not integrated into the total personality, which remains one-sided and restricted. The dark brother in the psyche may prove to be the source of instinctive energy that fuels the journey of individuation. When I arrived at the C.G. Jung Institute in Zürich to train as an analyst, I dreamt that my dark brother was sitting next to Jung at table and being treated by him with easy consideration. The anima/animus, which when unconscious, autonomous and projected, create such confusion in the world of personal relationships, when differentiated, fulfil their proper function as the linking principle to the treasure-house of the collective unconscious. When you stop imagining someone else is going to fulfil you, you may begin to fulfil yourself.

The withdrawal of the libido and interest that have gone into the love or hate of one's projected inner contents in others, means that energy is now made available for individuation. The heat that was formerly expended in the world of appearances forges a new centre of gravity which permits the psyche to right itself and regain its balance in the storms of life. To understand what withdrawal of projection feels like, imagine meeting again after many years someone you loved or hated intensely in your youth and discovering that you now have no feeling for that person and may even have forgotten their name.

When an individual ceases to identify so strongly with the outer world and his place in it, the split between inner world and outer world becomes less sharply defined. This sounds a high, far-off experience reserved for the great mystics who know that the microcosm reflects the macrocosm and for whom that which is above is the same as that which is below. It certainly sounds rather presumptuous for ordinary mortals to talk about the mysteries of what Jung, following the Medieval Schoolmen, called the 'Unus Mundus', the potential, pre-existent model of creation in the mind of God, in accordance with which God produced the phenomenal universe. Nevertheless, we have, I believe, all had some intimation of this oneness of inner and outer, actual and potential, in the experience of the meaningful coincidence or synchronicity. It is a momentary event which befalls us, and the matter of it may seem quite trivial, and yet it shocks us for a while into a different order of reality and arouses a strong emotional response, that is, until our conventional, rational attitudes succeed in throwing a wet blanket over it. Such an experience is an introduction to a state of awareness in which the normal laws of time, space and causality are suspended, a world where all potentialities coexist.

In order for such passing experiences to foster a new symbol-informed attitude and a new way of being-in-the-world, some conscious encounter with the archetypal forces of the collective unconscious would be necessary. "The world is a bridge; build not your house on it" runs an unknown logion of Jesus quoted by Akbar. To one side of the precarious bridge is the dangerous fall into the gulf of this-worldliness; to the other side lies the dark and bottomless chasm of the collective unconscious. There, the peril the soul faces is possession and submersion by encounter and identification with the archetypes. This is a frightening and unknown world whose paths few but the foolhardy or spiritually ambitious would choose to tread. St. Paul wrote ominously of it: "For we wrestle not against flesh and blood but against principalities, against powers, against the rulers of the darkness of this world, against spiritual wickedness in high places".

Nature does not take leaps and yet it is chiefly through shocks and crises that people develop. Not everyone has to take the shaman's night-sea journey of conscious confrontation with the principalities and powers – but all have to experience to some degree the archetypal turning-points during the changes and chances of this fleeting world – birth, puberty, falling in love, marriage, parenthood, illness, accident, rage, bliss, intoxication, war, pain, madness, natural disaster and death. These form part of the litany of human life through which our knowledge of ourselves is deepened and extended. The ego, if it allows life to become its teacher, is thereby relativized and assumes a Janus-role, facing the two worlds, which, according to Jung, are ultimately one in the self, the union of all the opposites.

In most of the great religions, there is a tradition relating to the Anthropos, the original man, who is at the same time the innermost being of the single individual and of all humanity. The principle is concisely expressed in Hinduism – Atman is Brahman; that art thou. In many myths the body of the original being is the material origin of the phenomenal world. Thus it would seem that the unity of being of the human race is an idea very closely related to that of the One World.

The term 'Unus Mundus' denotes a state in which all

potentialities eternally coexist and inner and outer are one. To attain the level of consciousness at which the full meaning of this word – knowing together – is realised, is the aim of philosophy and religion throughout the world and is known by many names – satori, samadhi, tao, enlightenment, gnosis, the fourth room, sat-chit-ananda, mysterium coniunctionis and the kingdom of heaven. For most of us it is only glimpsed in moments of synchronicity or in the heightened awareness that accompanies the experience of déjà vu, precognitive dreams, closeness to death or disaster, the numinosity of nature and the self-transcendence that sometimes happens in love-making. It always brings with it a taste of salvation, an inner assurance that, in the words of Julian of Norwich, "all manner of things shall be well".

In the Gnostic Gospel of Thomas, Jesus describes the necessary conditions for entry into this state*:

Jesus saw children who were being suckled. He said to his disciples "These children who are being suckled are like those who enter the Kingdom." They said to Him: "Shall we then, being children, enter the Kingdom?" Jesus said to them: "When you make the two one, and when you make the inner as the outer and the outer as the inner and the above as the below, and when you make the male and the female into a single one, so that the male will not be male and the female not be female, when you make eyes in the place of an eye . . . then you shall enter the Kingdom."

One pictorial symbolic language of mysterious origins, perhaps deriving like the Gospel of Thomas from the wisdom of Egypt and exuding something of the same atmosphere, which still speaks subtle truths to contemporary consciousness, is that of the Tarot. In its twenty-two arcana, representing the archetypal nodes on the journey of circumambulation round the centre that is the self, it is the summation of medieval Christian-alchemical teaching

*Logion 22, pp. 17 & 19, *The Gospel according to Thomas*, Collins, 1959

about the process of an individual's coming to be in the world. Perhaps it may even echo faintly the gnostic wisdom of Catharism that perished with the martyrs of Montségur but lived on in the hearts and minds of its secret devotees into the middle of the fourteenth century and beyond. The last trump, number twenty-one, the goal of the quest and the very dance itself, is called The World. It shows a beautiful naked woman of markedly androgynous form standing on one foot in a mandorla with the symbols of the evangelists or the fixed signs of the zodiac at the four corners.

There she is, at the centre of the turning world, motionlessly dancing all creatures into existence and out again, maintaining the elements in harmony, and luring man on to his journey of transformation. She is the union of heaven and earth, spirit and matter, the consciousness of the unconscious, the Anima Mundi or World-Soul who is equated with the original man and with Divine wisdom.

I have tried in a roundabout and allusive way to present the world as a vale of soul-making as well as a peril of the soul. Such matters cannot be discussed other than by paradox. The world is our *prima materia* and cannot just remain a *massa confusa*, without form and void. The spirit of transformation broods over its undifferentiated darkness and the seeds of the evolutionary principle are sown. But the evolutionary principle as a blind instinctive process stops with man. By conscious labour, trial and error and suffering, man is required to make the marriage of heaven and earth possible. To do this he must become aware of soul as his tabernacle, vehicle and wedding-garment.

The world, says Wittgenstein, is "all that is the case". Etymologically it derives from two words meaning 'the age of man', or the 'course of man's life'. The Greek and Latin words for 'world' mean 'order'. To Heraclitus the fiery Logos of the soul is the same as that which animates the world, and the Logos teaches that all things are one. If this be so, then individuation, far from isolating a man from his world, links his fate with the universal ordering principle. The course of a man's life, encountering and learning from all that is the case, can lead him to discover the order that is both himself and the world. Then he will have soul, and "to have soul", says Jung, "is the whole adventure of life".

Chapter 4

The many faces of consciousness

Self-transcendence and initiation

WHEN AND IN what circumstances is it admissible to use the term 'consciousness' other than as an attribute or function appertaining exclusively to the ego? In common usage it is notoriously hard to define, except in an arbitrarily limited or tautologous manner. If, for example, we say it is the state of being awake and alert, we thereby relegate many varieties of psychic experience to the realm of the unconscious. If, on the other hand, in a more specialised psychological sense, we confine it to the activity of the ego, we are little better off, since the ego is, by its own definition, the subject of consciousness. Furthermore, we should still have to face the questions of what should be included in the concept 'ego' and whether there may be states, more or less independent of ego-functioning, which fall within the category of consciousness.

Questions of this sort would not have troubled the birth of our word 'consciousness', a robust, tough-minded child of post-Reformation certitudes. It was coined in 1632 as a cognate form of the ambiguous 'conscience', meaning 'knowledge of which one has the testimony within oneself', as in "the consciousness of mine own wants". Nobody, at this period, questioned the ontological unity of the personality, so that the problem of ego-consciousness versus other varieties simply did not arise.

Much has happened in the intervening centuries to erode

the monolithic solidity of the concept. The Romantics interested themselves in the possibility of differing qualities of consciousness and experimented with psychedelic drugs. There is clearly a degree of discrepancy and discontinuity between Coleridge, the inspired poet who on "honey-dew hath fed" and Coleridge, the prosaic interlocutor of the person from Porlock.* But it was not until the scientific investigations of the Victorian era that the cracks finally began to show.

From the mid-nineteenth century, mediumism and occult phenomena attracted increasing scientific interest, as did the condition popularly known as split personality. The *Sydenham Lexicon of Medicine and Allied Sciences*, referring in 1882 to "double consciousness", defines it as "a condition which has been described as a double personality showing in some measure two separate and independent trains of thought and two independent mental capabilities in the same individual". Will the real ego please stand up?

Thanks to the work of Freud, it gradually came to be accepted by a majority of educated people in the West that the ego is not always king of the psychic castle but may be temporarily dethroned by other contents, dirty rascals with a life of their own, responsible for our Freudian slips. It was the aim of psychoanalysis, through the interpretation of dreams and free association, to unmask these hidden complexes of the unconscious, trace their origins in early childhood and depotentiate them, restoring to the ego its rightful primacy and enabling the patient to make a more satisfactory adaptation to the circumstances of his life. Freud's view of the unconscious was thus predominantly negative, and his professed aim that, where id was there ego shall be, strikes many people today as unduly imperialistic.

* *Kubla Khan or A Vision in Dream*; The Poems of Samuel Taylor Coleridge, Oxford University Press, London (1907)

That we now see the unconscious in a more kindly light is due in great measure to the pioneering work of Jung. During the period of his collaboration with Freud, when he coined the word 'complex' and provided, through his work on the Association Experiment, scientifically respectable evidence for the existence of such an entity, he was in full agreement that the ego is the highest psychic authority. Nevertheless, his background and experience contrasted sharply with those of Freud and were to lead him in a very different direction. He was, to begin with, aware from early childhood of what he called No. 1 and No. 2 personality both in himself and in his mother,* and saw that each had its value and validity. Then, too, in his doctoral thesis, which antedates the influence of Freud, *On the Psychology and Pathology of So-Called Occult Phenomena*, he investigates a case of mediumism, in which some of the sub-personalities that reveal themselves exhibit positive qualities inaccessible to the subject's conscious ego. By 1945, his experience had led him to the point where he could say, to an audience of Swiss doctors: ". . . the real and authentic psyche is the unconscious, whereas the ego-consciousness can only be regarded as a temporary epiphenomenon."†

In his view that over-identification with ego-consciousness is a serious problem facing modern man rather than our crowning glory, Jung is, in terms of psychiatry and clinical psychology, a dangerous and radical revolutionary. From the point of view of religion, on the other hand, he is at one with mystical theology at all times and in all places. According to tradition, attachment to the ego and its aims is the greatest obstacle to the unitive knowledge of God. This apparently paradoxical, experimental knowledge is succinctly expressed by St. Paul's

* *Memories, Dreams, Reflections*, Routledge & Kegan Paul Plc (1963)
† *C.W.* Vol. 16, para. 205

"I live, now not I, but Christ in me."* Pascal's "Le moi est haïssable"† is no mere moralistic platitude or piece of pious rhetoric. It is the disgust with the ordinary mode of functioning and state of consciousness expressed throughout the ages by psalmist, prophet and saint following a transcendental experience. The subject is conscious during such an experience but, it would appear, not with the everyday consciousness of the ego.

There is a good case for stating that the main purpose of Christianity is to provide the means and create the conditions for self-transcendence. The Church today, however, shows a curious lack of interest about the psychological and ontological implications of its mystical tradition and, when it comes to calling the faithful to the interior life, its trumpet gives an uncertain sound.

It is, in fact, chiefly through the medium of the Eastern religions and their offshoots that ideas concerning the nature of consciousness and its different levels have become matters of general knowledge in the West. The minimum working hypothesis of Vedanta‡, which Aldous Huxley and Isherwood did so much to popularise in the post-war period, postulates:

1 Man's real nature is divine.
2 His purpose on earth is to realise that divine nature.
3 All religions are essentially in agreement.

But the Hindu formulation on which this is based: "Atman is Brahman; That art Thou", when received theoretically by minds that are unprepared, produces either incomprehension or a dangerous inflation in which the ego identifies with the Self.

Buddhism radically undermines the presuppositions of a

---

* *Galatians*, II, 20
† *Pensées et Opuscules*, Blaise Pascal, ed. Brunschvicg, p. 541, pensée 455, Hachette, Paris (1912)
‡ *Vedanta for the Western World*, ed. Christopher Isherwood, Marcel Rodd. Co., Hollywood, New York (1946)

materialistic, egocentric attitude by presenting the ego as an illusion which binds us to an existence of meaningless willing and striving in an illusory universe. The total sacrifice of one's habitual sense of identity and the denial of any real continuity of consciousness implicit in such a teaching has proved too radical a solution to the problems of the human condition for most people in the West. Certainly, Jung was not in favour of discarding too lightly our hard-won ego-consciousness. His position is, perhaps, best expressed in one of his favourite Latin tags: "Mercurius duplex, utriusque capax" (Mercury is two-fold, able to grasp both the one and the other).

The other major attack on the assumptions of sense-based ego-consciousness comes from an unexpected source – physics. The classical principle of causality has long since been abandoned, along with the comprehensible nineteenth-century model of the universe. Now it appears that there is no one-to-one correspondence between reality and theory, indeed that the nature of reality may elude altogether the grasp of rational understanding. As a result, physicists are faced with problems which only a few years ago would have been considered metaphysical. But, as physics moves ever further from the world of the senses to converge with the mysteries of the East, the rest of the world soldiers on as though quantum mechanics had never occurred, as unmoved by its amazing revelations as earlier generations were by the ecstasies of St. John of the Cross or the speculations of Parmenides.

Even those professionally involved in the care of souls are not immune to resistance when it comes to relinquishing time-honoured notions of reality. Patient and psychiatrist alike are expected to function normally in a rational, Apollonian light, fully orientated as to space and time, whatever physicists may say about these. It is also best to harbour no doubts about one's own identity or that of others. The capacity to plan a project and carry it through – goal orientated, purposeful activity – is further useful evidence of sanity. In fact, health of mind is equivalent to adequate functioning of the ego, in accord with the conventions of one's society. As a rule of thumb, such a way of looking at things has many advantages, but it fails to take into account the need for the ego to be relativised if psychic growth is to take place. As a result, we hasten to try and cure so-called nervous breakdowns and psychotic episodes without asking ourselves whether such conditions may have a potentially positive part to play within the individuation process.

During the early years of the century Jung surprised his colleagues by spending hours a day actually watching and listening to the schizophrenic patients in the Burghölzli Hospital in Zürich, as though what they did and said might actually have some meaning. His observations showed him not only that ritualised gestures might indeed throw some light on the patient's condition, but that some statements revealed knowledge of, for instance, ancient mithraic liturgies, that could not have been part of the conscious ego's memory. It is, of course, almost impossible to offer scientific proof in such matters, but many people report similar occurrences. I was once part of a group attending a clinical demonstration at a mental hospital and heard a schizophrenic patient recounting a typical delusional system. One feature of this was that the world is gradually being taken over by beings who look human but have jaguar souls. Several years later I read an anthropological report about a recently investigated tribe of South American Indians who professed, not without some justification, an identical belief. It was experiences like this that led Jung to formulate his hypothesis of the collective unconscious. An encounter with the archetypal contents of this realm may shatter the unprepared ego, but, in other circumstances, may bring healing. If schizophrenia is, as Jung thought, an initiation that failed, may not some of the failures be due to the inability of the initiate's environment to accommodate non-ego experiences?

That it is possible to raise the success rate of the initiations, has been demonstrated by, amongst others, a colleague of Jung's, Professor J.W. Perry*, who established a clinic in San Francisco for the specialised treatment of schizophrenia. Each patient, on admission, was accompanied for as long as necessary by a non-medical helper whose function was to listen sympathetically and help the patient to see what was happening as an important stage in the individuation process. Within one to five days most instances of bizarre behaviour ceased and, within three months, almost all the patients (initiates?) were able to leave the clinic and re-adjust to their lives, eighty-five percent making a good recovery. Drugs and other forms of physical therapy or restraint were not employed.

The encounter with the numinous can madden or transform, and myths often point to this psychic power which both destroys and heals. We have so far been considering consciousness in its own terms, in lexicons and scientific texts, historically, rationally and critically. The time has now come to look at it from the other side, and to see how it appears to the 'unconscious'. In individuals, the dream provides a non-ego commentary, often contrapuntal, on the attitudes and performance of the conscious subject. It seems possible that myth and religion are, to the societies from which they spring, like 'big dreams' in the life of the individual. The statements they make, whether or not they refer to actual events in the phenomenal world or to metaphysical truths, could therefore be considered as symbolic representations of psychic processes. With this in mind, let us examine two familiar myths, one Hebrew, one Greek, both central to European culture, which seem to relate to the birth and nature of consciousness.

* *Methods of Treatment in Analytical Psychology*, ed. Ian F. Baker, Verlag Adolf Bonz – D. Fellback (1980) and also *The Far Side of Madness*, J.W. Perry, Spectrum Books (1947)

But before doing this, we should be aware that to enter the world of myth is in itself to risk a relativisation, perhaps salutary, of the ego. Once down the rabbit-hole or through the looking-glass, things are not always what they seem, and the ego's binary categories are inadequate. An indispensable companion on the journey we shall be undertaking is Jung's double Mercurius, guide of souls and patron of alchemists. As Hermes, he is the author of secret hermetic revelations from the other side of consciousness, as well as of the hermeneutic necessary for their interpretation. He represents a subtle (> sub tela: under the weave) mode of intelligence (> inter-lego: choose between) that can operate on both sides of the consciousness threshold. He is, in alchemy, cause and effect of the union of sun and moon, a linking principle in the cosmos which manifests as spirit-matter, male-female, young-old, good-evil, conscious-unconscious. As trickster and shapeshifter, he can, like Puck and Ariel, appear in any form, without being thereby pinned down or defined. His is a world not of either-or but of both-and, even of not-this-not-that.

Creation by division: the Fall

The first myth for which we shall be invoking his help, the Creation theme from the *Book of Genesis*, is too well-known to need re-telling here in detail. All that is necessary is to recall the salient features. To begin with, there are two creation myths involved, with different names for God. The first, an account of the labours performed on the six primal days, with a sabbath on the seventh, seems to refer to an ideal creation in the mind of God, in which everything was "very good". But it is to the second creation (*Genesis* II, 4 – III, 24), which tells of the transgression by which the man and the woman "stepped across" out of paradise into incarnation and generation that we shall be directing our attention. Its main stages are:

1 God makes man out of dust to look after the garden he is planning.
2 God tells the man he may eat from any tree he likes except the tree of knowledge of good and evil. On the day he eats of that tree he will die.
3 God decides to make for man "an help meet for him".
4 First he makes all the creatures and brings them to the man to see what he will call them.
5 He causes a deep sleep to fall upon the man and makes woman from one of his ribs. Hence man and woman are really one flesh.
6 The serpent "more subtil than any beast of the field" persuades the woman to eat of the tree of knowledge of good and evil, and she tempts the man.
7 Consequences – awareness of nakedness, confrontation with God, sentencing of the sinners, expulsion from the garden.

If we view this story hermetically and not through a network of religious and moral associations dating back to Sunday school, various points stand out as worthy of comment or inquiry. It would appear that God is making man for his own purposes as a tiller of the earth. These purposes do not include conscious intelligence (knowledge of good and evil); it is enough that he has power over the rest of creation in accordance with God's will. Woman is not made from the dust of the earth like man, but is formed out of his deep sleep and the integument of his heart and lungs. This God of Eden does not seem to know all that goes on in his garden. There is an autonomous content, the serpent (created by this God?) who possesses special knowledge about life, death, man, woman and consciousness. The serpent has presumably its own reasons for wishing the primal couple to become conscious and leave their paradisal home. The woman becomes the agent of consciousness for the man. The first result of consciousness is the awareness of sexual differences between these two halves of one erstwhile whole. God, we note, is not the only god, and already shows signs of his later notorious jealousy: "Man is become as one of us, to know good and evil". God's slip-up can be interpreted in three possible ways:

1   He may be hopelessly split like Wotan in "Die Walküre", the victim of a war between two contradictory intentions in himself (his right and left hands?).

2   He is fully in charge of things, a Machiavellian god who intends the fruit to be eaten, draws the man's attention to the tree on purpose and creates the serpent and the woman to bring about the "felix culpa" or fruitful sin.

3   There are other powers at work which transcend this god and of which he may even be ignorant. (Who, for instance, is that God in *Genesis* I?)

Let us, for the moment, leave this three-fold question at the back of our minds and go on to consider the nature of the punishment meted out by Yahweh to his unruly creatures. The curse of Adam is work. He is to be forcibly reminded of his own earthly origins by the obligation to earn his bread from the bramble- and thistle-infested ground and eat it in sorrow until he returns to the dust at death. The punishment of Eve and the serpent is inter-related and more subtle. The penalty for their fatal collusion is that they shall be set at odds with one another. Eve is to be kept so busy painfully bringing forth and raising children, in addition to serving the interests of her earthy mate, that she will have no time or energy left over for serpentine speculations concerning humanity's true nature and origin, or for developing the potentiality for discrimination which is now its heritage. The effects of this legend on the deformation of human conscience within a patriarchal society can scarcely be over-estimated. Woman, instead of being associated with the creative curiosity which leads along the path of individuation, has been equated with sin, sex, matter and body, deceit and death and, in consequence, has been repressed by the patriarchy and at the same time expected to crush the serpent's head. To this day, it is the careful, ever-busy Martha who presides, martyred and maternal, over human relationships, in the depth of woman's guilty conscience and man's expecations. The very designation, "Eve", as mother of all living things, is one of the effects of the Fall.

If the Judaic tradition subjugates the dangerously subtle feminine principle to the earthy masculine one, does the other great religion of our Western civilisation do any-thing to validate the impartial workings of consciousness and free it from the loaded dice of the post-Edenic conscience? At first glance, the myths of Greece, with their wealth of goddesses, offer a far greater variety of models for feminine patterns of behaviour than Mother Eve. But if we restrict ourselves to a consideration of the myth which, above all others, seems to refer to the birth of consciousness and its consequences (the story of Prom-etheus) then the attitude towards women it displays is even more hostile than that of *Genesis*.

The tale is more complex than that of Adam and Eve as there are many variants and no one authorised version, but the main elements are as follows. Gods and men were of common origin. Prometheus seems to stand between the two and to be the agent of their separation. Sometimes he and his brother, Epimetheus, are presented as the first men, and sometimes he seems to be another form of Hephaistos, a crafty smith-god and son of Hera, who played midwife at the birth of Athene from the head of Zeus, and fashioned the race of ash-men who came to people the earth. In some versions, his brother Epithemeus ("after-thought", or "he who learns only from the event"), lavished all the gifts of the gods on the animals, so that man was left with nothing. Out of compassion, Prom-etheus ("fore-thinker") stole fire, either from the forge of

Hephaistos, from the flame of Zeus on Olympus or from the sun itself, and, keeping it alight in the stalk of a giant fennel, brought it back to compensate for man's deprivation. Zeus wreaks vengeance on the thief and on the race of men. Prometheus is impaled, nailed and chained, far from the haunts of men on the highest peak of the Caucasus, tormented by an eagle which comes daily to devour his liver that grows again every night until, in the fullness of time, he is freed by the hero, Herakles. To punish man, Zeus bids Hephaistos (or Prometheus himself) to fashion from the earth the beautiful woman, Pandora, in the image of the immortal goddesses, who each bestow on her a gift. The gods, too, play their part. Hermes endows her with his own duplicity and presents her to the simple Epimetheus who, heedless of his brother's warning, falls victim to desire and weds her. Her dowry is a box from Zeus, filled with sickness, death and all the evils with which mankind is afflicted, which issue forth as soon as the lid is opened. All that remains within is hope. According to another story, it is the newly-arisen woman who, overcome by curiosity, opens up the receptacle and lets slip the baneful contents.

Points to note. Prometheus, "he of the crooked thoughts" plays a Luciferian role, not unlike that of the serpent. He seems to be more cunning than the god in charge, plays a trick on him, apparently wins and is then apparently defeated. The enlightenment he brings, like Eve's apple, creates consciousness along with sexuality, and instils the fear of concupiscence. We can look beyond Freud for the phallic significance of the sparks within the hollow stem of the giant fennel, for this plant, the narthex, furnished the wands carried in the Bacchanalian procession. The new fire is brought up from the shrine of the Black Virgin of Marseilles at Candlemas, the feast which replaces the orgiastic rites of Demeter and Persephone, one of the titles of Our Lady of Marseilles, Notre Dame de Fenouil (fennel) is said to derive from the Provençal

'Feu-Nou' (new fire). Fennel also provided the boxes used by physicians to carry their healing unguents and, by extension, the word used for books on the cure of diseases. Prometheus, unlike the serpent in *Genesis*, is the creator of human beings as well as their benefactor. This fact, combined with his assistance at the birth of Athene, divine wisdom, from the All-Father, should be borne in mind when we come to consider the Gnostic creation myths which synthesize the traditions of Israel and Greece. Prometheus' punishment, a sort of crucifixion through which he is suspended between gods and men until the end of the age, includes the perpetual gnawing of the liver, the seat of the emotions, especially love, though secreting as well the gall of bitterness. Shakespeare furnished amplification that resonates in a curiously apposite way: "This is the liver-vein which makes the flesh a deity."*

The two most important factors which *Genesis* and the Prometheus myth have in common concern the apparent mistake of the gods in allowing man to acquire consciousness, and the proposition that evil came into the world through and with woman. Consciousness is a divine attribute not intended for human consumption. When man achieves it, he also brings about a separation from God or the gods. Or, one could say, he forgets that his real nature is divine, and becomes the victim of sensual thinking. Woman, though ostensibly the origin of evil, is, in fact, full of ambiguity. To begin with, is Pandora's name, "all the gifts", purely ironical, or does it refer to the bountiful earth herself, whose gifts are positive or negative, depending on the use to which man puts them? Might not a hermetic reading of the myths suggest that the material for the work of transformation, the realisation of the potential for consciousness which the serpent hints at, is to be found in human sexuality and the problems of relationship between man and woman? One might also

* *Love's Labour's Lost*, IV, 3

surmise that the hostility one finds against the feminine in myths illustrates woman's vital role in releasing paradoxical feelings in man.

Herakles, as champion of the self

The greatest of the Greek heroes, Herakles, bears a name which means "glory of Hera". If we may assume, without having to reformulate the validity of the idea, implicit in Jung's writings, that the hero is the symbol for the ego engaged in the individuation process, then it is important to examine who provides the hero with the opportunity for self-realisation, who is the real source of his heroic deeds.

His deadly opponent is, from the outset, Hera, the goddess of marriage. From jealousy, she thwarts the intention of Zeus, his father, that he should be a great king, by delaying the hour of his birth. As a result, he finds himself bound to the service of Eurystheus, his future royal task-master, born an hour before him. All these tasks have been interpreted as a striving, in different forms, against the terrible mother whose archetype is both destructive and life-giving. The conflict of Herakles with the breast of Hera is made explicit in the myth. On one occasion, he wounds it with an arrow; on another, in suckling, he causes her such pain that she pulls him from her, releasing a flood of milk that is the origin of the Milky Way, the route along which deities become constellated and heroes pursue their pilgrim path.

The myth of Herakles, the thrice-born, can be divided into three stages of initiation. In the first, the hero, freeing himself from the constraints of family life and education, glories in the exuberance of his masculine strength, lustful for life and killing, fathering a host of sons, massacring his foes mercilessly and indiscriminately. In the second stage, that of the Labours, he finds himself forced to serve a man he considers inferior, travelling north, south, east, west and down to Hades itself, ridding the world of monsters and afflictions and performing tasks of expiation for the one-sidedness of his youthful folly and the murder of his own children. The third stage relates explicitly to the need for reconciliation of the masculine and feminine principles in the individuation process.

At the completion of his labours, following another bout of madness, Herakles is sold in slavery to Queen Omphale, who dresses him in women's clothes and makes him learn the traditional feminine crafts. After three years he is set free and seeks and wins a bride of his own choosing, Deianeira. But something of his autonomous, instinctual wildness apparently remains. At an important rite of passage, a river-crossing, he fails to carry his wife, entrusting her to the centaur, Nessus, who molests her sexually. Herakles dispatches him with one arrow, but the scene has been set for his final initiation.

This lapse leads to the ultimate reconciliation between Herakles and Hera. He tries to regain his former wife, Iole – a regression to an earlier stage of anima development – and receives from Deianeira the burning, irremovable shirt of Nessus.

Herakles sacrifices himself in the purifying flames of a pyre lit by himself and is raised to Olympus. There he undergoes a ritual of rebirth to become fully and finally Hera's son, after which he is united to the goddess in the renewed form of her daughter. His image is also set among the stars.

A Gnostic alternative to orthodox belief

In pursuit of our theme concerning the nature of consciousness, and, in particular, the role played by the feminine principle in its development, we must now move forward from the myths of classical Greece and the scriptures of the Old Testament to consider a less familiar world where these two streams converged. For five centuries a tradition existed which linked ancient Egypt to modern Christianity – Isis to Mary – through the medium of Helleno-Jewish syncretism. This synthesis had already been at work for 250 years by the time Christianity appeared in the great crucible that was Alexandria.

A major landmark in this process was the translation of the Hebrew bible into Greek, in the influential version known as the *Septuagint*, commissioned for the great library of Alexandria by Ptolemy Philadelphus (325–246 BC). By the time the New Testament came to be written – in Greek – there already existed a whole literature employing the concepts and ideas which, used by St. Paul and St. John, became the basis of Christian theology. The major extant source is to be found in the extensive work of Philo of Alexandria who died c. 50 AD. Although he was a loyal Jew, the Alexandrian zeitgeist forced him, as it had Aristobulus two centuries earlier, to face the philosophical problems posed by Judaism's encounter with Platonism, of man's relation to a finite, temporal eternal, good God. His monotheism precluded neither belief in intermediate spiritual beings, nor the acknowledgement of the existence of divinised supermen like Isaac or Moses but, ultimately, a gulf remains. This is bridged, according to Philo, from God's side, by the unique Logos, his first-born son and stream of his radiation, interpreter, prophet, High Priest, intermediary, shepherd, fountain of wisdom, principle of unity and stability of the universe, senior to all the angels, relating, as third member of a trinity of divine powers, to the authority and the goodness of God. Thus it is through the Logos that man can come to the knowledge of God; when Rebecca, like Sarah, an image of the archetypal feminine principle, seen interchangeably as Virtue or Wisdom, draws water for the servant of Isaac, it is the Logos itself that he receives.

It is not necessary to underline the resemblances

between such teaching and the language of the *New Testament*, but it is worth noting that Philo was the originator of the word 'archetype', which Jung was to pick up and employ so creatively. Also, the school of archetypal wisdom to which he belonged, which had already given birth to the *Wisdom of Solomon*, with its vision of a hypostatized Sophia as the emanation of the beauty and the power of God, was an acknowledged source for the Christian catechetical school of St. Clement of Alexandria and Origen which flourished at the end of the second century.

In the century or so which separates Philo from Pantaenus, the founder of the Catechetical School, a somewhat mysterious figure who was reputed to have visited India, a surprising gap exists in Alexandria, the intellectual and cultural power-house of the world. Apart from the *Epistle to the Hebrews*, which is attributed to an Alexandrian source, there are no authoritative works from the pens of great teachers as might have been expected from the city with the largest and most learned Jewish population, and thus an ideal seed-bed for Christian evangelisation. The answer to the question this poses, we now know, is that great teachers, producing works of remarkable depth and subtlety, did indeed exist during that silent century in Alexandria.

In the teachings of the Gnostics a glimpse of the true feminine inner consciousness came into the world, but their doctrine was considered heretical by the procrustean standards of post-conciliar orthodoxy and destroyed. It is now possible to state, with some confidence, that in the first century and a half of its existence, when it was spreading like wildfire throughout the Roman Empire and beyond, Christianity, as it manifested in Egypt, was largely indistinguishable from what was later defined as the heresy of Gnosticism.

In fact, the orthodox Fathers of the Church found Gnosticism extremely hard to define, as it is more an attitude and an atmosphere than a specific body or doctrine. It is not a philosophy – the use of discursive reasoning in the investigation of being, knowledge and right conduct is quite alien to the interests of Gnostics, who were, however, great lovers of wisdom. Neither is it a religion in the exoteric sense, in so far as it is generally unconcerned with faith and morals and is not based on belief in a hypothetical divine principle or on subscription to a set of theoretical propositions. It is, rather, based on experimental knowledge, gnosis, of the transcendental, and should be seen as what Professor Quispel has called "the mythologisation of a Self-experience". It follows from this that there is no central institution or body of homogeneous doctrine that can be called Gnostic. The great Gnostic teachers were freelance speculative theologians and spiritual directors who, unencumbered by exterior dogmatic norms, developed their ideas in the direction that their own interests, qualifications and inspirations dictated, within a loose context that was patent of Christian interpretation. Until recently, our knowledge of Gnosticism has depended almost entirely on the polemical writings of its bitterest enemies, Christian apologists and defenders of the faith, like Irenaeus and Ephiphanius. Over the past two centuries, however, occasional fragments and codices of the lost world of Gnosticism have emerged from the sands of time. Most had to wait a long time for translation and penetrated no further into public consciousness than the pages of some learned journal.

This situation has now been transformed, thanks to the discovery in 1945 of the Gnostic library at Nag Hammadi, in Egypt, near the site of the first Christian monastery, and the eventual translation and publication of its fifty-two texts in 1977. The implications of this event have not yet been grasped by the educated public, the major one being that, from the beginning, there was an influential school of Christianity that was almost entirely Gnostic in outlook.

The main reasons for this lack of impact are two. Firstly, Gnostic literature, though often sublime, can be extremely complicated and difficult to read, sometimes sounding like a mixture between a schizophrenic case report and a charismatic service. Here, for example, is a verse from *The Discourse on the Eighth and the Ninth*, a Nag Hammadi codex*:

He is perfect, the invisible God to whom one speaks in silence – his image is moved when it is directed, and it governs – the one mighty in power, who is exalted above majesty, who is better than the honoured ones, Zoxazoth a *oo* ee *ooo eee ooo ee oooooo* ooooo *oooooo* uuuuuu *oooooooooooo ooo* Zozazoth.

A second major reason for the neglect of Gnosticism has been the psychological gulf separating the academics, most of them card-carrying Christians, theologians with a specialised knowledge of Coptic, Syriac, etc., who have been mainly responsible for such translations as exist, from the texts they were elucidating. Thus, "Metropator", a Gnostic name for the deity, which makes good psychological sense when rendered as "Mother/Father", was unsympathetically rendered as "maternal grandfather" by a famous scholar of an earlier period. Even today, one of the most important Gnostic texts has been translated with the resounding title of *The Hypostasis of the Archons*, which must make it somewhat remote from the concerns of most potential readers, whereas *The Reality of the Rulers* might elicit some interesting questions – "Who are these real rulers? Have they anything to do with me?"

Because of the great variety and complexity of Gnostic writings, I shall not base myself on any one text in attempting to present what I nevertheless consider to be a characteristically Gnostic allegorical summary of the creation story in *Genesis*. The stages in that story viewed through Gnostic eyes might look something like this: the

* *The Nag Hammadi Library in English*, ed. James M. Robinson, E.J. Brill, Leiden (1977)

divine source of all, sometimes called Depth, is the unknowable one, whose ineffability is expressed in the dictum of Basilides:

The non-existent God, created the non-existent universe out of the non-existent.

There proceeded, nevertheless, from this source, an outflowing of creative energy that is often designated as the feminine First Thought, Ennoia. In another system, Depth and Silence bring forth Mind and Truth, whence emanate further syzygies or divine couples. The last of the Aeons, the thirteenth, unpaired, Sophia, Wisdom, yearns to return to the unknown source and, unable to cross the threshold, undergoes a "fall", as a result of which the phenomenal world comes into existence. The ruler of this world, the demiurge, foolish god of the blind, believes himself to be the creator of all. Assisted by his fellow archons, he makes man from the earth, a weak, horizontal creature who cannot stand upright. Sophia has pity on man and infuses her spirit into him so that he can raise himself off the ground and not remain wholly subject to the rulers. This spirit is externalised in the form of woman, and also manifests as the tree and the serpent, to set humanity on its evolutionary path by encouraging rebellion against the tyrant ego. Adam and Eve are expelled from the garden, and the feminine spirit, still longing, from within its physical prison, to know its true origin and return thence, suffers unspeakable degradations whilst awaiting the hero who brings redemption.

Having discussed consciousness from the standpoint of the conscious ego and commented on it in the light of myth, let us explore the possibilities of the Gnostic approach, thinking around and within the subject as the spirit moves, permitting connections to make themselves as and how they will.

The fall of Sophia – a neo-Gnostic meditation

To Gnostics the archetypes were not just concepts or abstract ideas, nor were they quite the same as the gods of old, personifications of human instincts and receptacles for human projections, who were already entering into their twilight by the time Gnosticism appeared on the scene. It seems as though some Gnostics, at least, came very near to understanding the archetypes as psychoid, that is, subliminal, collective, autonomous energy quanta, manifesting typically in synchronistic or transcendental experiences, possessing individuals and operating through them. The closeness of their views to his own impressed Jung greatly, though, when he died, only a fraction of the Nag Hammadi library, the Jung Codex, had been translated. The somewhat esoteric aspect of Jung's work on synchronicity and the paranormal, together with his remarkable Gnostic book, *Septem Sermones ad Mortuos** which appeared during his encounter with the collective unconscious in 1916, "written by Basilides in Alexandria, the city where the East toucheth the West", has, so far, aroused surprisingly little public interest amongst students of analytical psychology. This may be due in part to the style of such writings which is often repellent, both portentous and sententious, and necessitates a jarring leap from the normal mode in which ego discussions are conducted.

The unknown God . . . the undiscovered self. Christ the Gnostic: "I know whence I came, and whither I go." Our little life is rounded with a sleep. Knowing-about and gnosis. Montaigne's *"Que sais-je?"*. The Gnostic affirmation, "I am the child of earth and starry heaven". It's a wise child that knows its own father. We choose our own parents to provide us

* Stuart & Watkins, London (1967)

with the greatest opportunity of resolving our karmic inheritance and reaching enlightenment. The unconscious really is unconscious, and the archetypes really are irrepresentable in themselves. Harpocrates with finger to lip. The insensitive man praises silence in a torrent of words. Vere tu es deus absconditus.

God's wisdom, grace, thought, spirit. Pistis Sophia above, Sophia Zoe, the wisdom of the life-force, striving from below. "The Lord possessed me in the beginning of his way, before his works of old. I was set up from everlasting, from the beginning . . . I was daily his delight, rejoicing always before him." This spirit enters the human psyche and appears first as hubris, the overweening belief in one's own powers to comprehend all with the mind. The wet, winding, left-hand path is to follow Sophia on the return journey from Chaos to where she belongs, beyond the planetary spheres. Simon Magus, "the father of all heresies", simplifies and unites the tale of the two Sophias:

In the beginning the Father planned to create angels and arch-angels.
His thought leaped forth from him, knowing her Father's will;
She descended to the lower regions.
She generated angels and powers, by whom this world was made.
But after she generated them, she was held captive by them.
She suffered every disgrace from them,
So that she could not return to her Father,
She was even imprisoned in a human body,
And through all ages passed as from vessel to vessel,
Into one female body after another . . .
Last of all she was manifest in a prostitute;
This is the lost sheep.

Brahma breathes out: Brahma breathes in. Spirit is

breath, and in Hebrew is feminine. The Spirit of God hovers over the waters of Chaos in which her reflected image initiates the process of transformation and incarnation. Helen, the lost Eve, is recognised by Simon Magus in a brothel in Tyre and redeemed by him. The theme of the redeemed redeemer. Jesus and the Magdalen. The Virgin and the Whore – two poles of the feminine archetype. Not just a hostile slander that Jesus was the son of a whore. With Mary's "Ave", the Eva cycle is fulfilled, but the whole was not redeemed. The Virgin is assumed bodily and crowned by the Son, but the Magdalen is still the lost sheep and still, as the Black Virgin, the secret, dark wisdom of the serpent, sells herself to all who desire her. Mary Magdalen, patron of penitents. Repentance as 'metanoia', change of attitude, transformation of mind. The Holy Ghost as the breast of God, sharing her symbol, the dove, with Aphrodite. Jesus tells of his mother, the Holy Spirit, taking him up to the great mountain, Tabor. Consciousness and love reconciled; thought and feeling, Eros and Logos, no longer opposed at the Sophia state of consciousness. The integrated animus as Sophia, intelligence expressed through relatedness.

"God who is our home." The many resting-places (mansions) are already in my Father's house. The Way is a circle, the stages are different modes of consciousness, none better or worse than any other. The wise old man is not necessarily superior to the eternal youth. To see the individuation process as a circumambulation strikes at the roots of spiritual pride. The serpent Ouroboros biting its tail is not just the mother complex from which we struggle to be free, it is the secret that in my end is my beginning. God – the circle whose centre is everywhere and circumference nowhere. To know these things theoretically or too soon is a stumbling-block on the

Way, the journey of soul-making, Psyche's search for
Eros. Projection makes the world go round. "Were it
not for the leaping and twinkling of the soul", writes
Jung, "man would rot away in his greatest passion,
idleness."*

But "Our hearts were made for God and will not
rest save in him."

The ruler of this world of ego-consciousness is, on the
other hand, a blind, foolish god. It is the necessary fate of
all to fall into multiplicity, into ignorance that is called
knowledge, into the way of opinion, carnal thinking, that
takes the world of appearances as the only reality. The
average sensual man, trained and conditioned by other
average sensual men, sensibly adapts to a life that leads
only to death in a world likewise doomed to extinction,
and sensibly decides to go quietly. The ego mode of
consciousness is not only a personal phenomenon, but
derives from collective attitudes which it in turn rein-
forces. The ego-persona system derives from the store of
public knowledge and the received ideas based on it that
are held to be correct at any historical period. To reject
these ideas and place one's own experimental gnosis above
that knowledge is always dangerous. Heraclitus regretted
that, though all men have the logos within them, they
prefer to follow opinion. The fate of heretics from
Socrates to Solzhenitsyn hardly encourages them to do
otherwise. The ego, like the demiurge, imagines itself to
be the sole ruler of its cosmos and brooks no insubordina-
tion from other psychic contents. It knows nothing of the
pre-conscious self, or what its face was like before it was
born. A baby has no ego and yet is an individual whole in
itself, containing a multitude of genetic potentialities, only
a minute proportion of which will ever be cultivated. One
day it begins to say "I", and the ego is born, to exist at first

---

* *Collected Works*, Vol IX, Part I, para. 56

only in islands of consciousness, but, through growing awareness of a separate physical reality and identication with the body, the ego-mode becomes more continuous. It casts the shades of the prison-house which obscure early childhood's intimations of immortality. In this process, words, the tools *par excellence* for constructing consciousness, become, paradoxically, the very bars of the prison-house. After Adam had named all the animals, God caused a deep sleep to fall upon him. The naming of things fosters the delusion that we know them, and so we cease experiencing them directly as in early childhood with the doors of perception cleansed, but perceive them dimly through a haze of verbal associations and memories.

The rulers, the planetary gods (planet or planē = error) who assist the demiurge in the creation of horizontal man keep him unaware of his true origin. They are the archetypal core of the complexes or sub-personalities that live our lives for us while we remain unconscious of them. If we become aware of them, they can fulfil their true function as channels along which energy can flow for the purposes of self-knowledge and self-fulfilment.

The ego-consciousness which emerges is that of the demiurge, and his limited perceptions are accounted the sole reality.

Man is a prisoner of space and time. His rulers are real, not only as the divisions of the week but as the complexes. The sun, the ego-complex, the chief ruler, rules the day, and, with its light and heat, blots out the hidden influence of the other archons. The moon is the great pendulum which keeps everything as it is, ticking over regularly, inexorably fixated within its own cycle. Its phases restrict self-expression to the pre-existent roles of girl, mother and old woman and man's response to these roles. Conception, birth, puberty, reproduction, death; the tide ebbs and flows; maid, wife and crone; as it was, is now and ever shall be. The devastating moon-consciousness which knows that all man's posturings and self-important exploits will pass away in the endless cycles of time as a child's sandcastle vanishes beneath the waves, this is the mother mode that lulls a man to sleep and denies him his chance to find himself through making his own mistakes. Mercury, if we relate to him correctly, may be the god who guides our journey. As an autonomous archetype, one of the planetary gods, he is the multi-sidedness of intelligence – one feels either stupid or clever, and compares how one feels with one's imaginary version of others. His, too, is the trite intellectualism that impedes understanding. Venus is the archetype inspiring love and sex, while Mars rules the adrenalin's will to win, and the primal rage, hidden within all, that they did not obtain from their childhood environment what was needful for their essential development. Jupiter can be the archetype of expansion and growth in wisdom or a complex core, inducing manic inflation and over-confidence. Saturn is our awareness of limitation and the melancholy that results from this, inducing feelings of inferiority, hopelessness and self-destruction in whose school the soul learns how sweet are the uses of adversity. The archetypes and complexes are not figures of speech but divine or demonic influences that, popping up when unconsciously invited like a genie from a bottle, take over and possess an individual. There can be no theoretical list of all the archetypes. Each person must discover his own devils by experience and by unmasking and naming them, allowing them to assume their proper place within the economy of the psyche and, perhaps, even, show themselves as holy daimons who befriend the soul in search of love.

The less we know of the rulers and the more repressed they are, the more likely they are to arise and overwhelm us, if not intra-psychically, then through physical symptoms or by means of external events, accidents and the behaviour of others who live out our unconsciousness for us. If, through the encounter with them, the ego relaxes his rigid control, then they may become channels along which energy can flow naturally and appropriately, modes of consciousness through which we can express ourselves and come to know our many-sidedness without panicky loss of identity. I do not believe that this is a description of the ego integrating or assimilating the other psychic contents, but if it is, then the ego that emerges from the process is so transformed as to merit another name. The acquisition of another name in baptism, reminds us that we are not just the result of parental complexes. This is also the significance of taking a new name in religion, the equivalent of finding a white stone with one's name on it. Avidya, ignorance, is the real sin to Gnostics, not knowing who one is.

Dismemberment, analysis of oneself, must precede self-remembering – the myth of the prodigal son. The feminine principle in the individuation process, Sophia, infuses her spirit into man. "Oh Grace! After these things I give thanks by singing a hymn to thee. For I have received life from thee when thou madest me wise. I praise thee. I call thy name which is hidden within me." In this passage from the Nag Hammadi document *The Discourse on the Eighth and Ninth*, Grace seems to be equated with Sophia herself, who reveals to man a world beyond that of the seven planetary archons and free from their power. Sophia is so often associated with virgin goddesses like Athene, goddess of wisdom, that it is well to remind ourselves that she is also called Prunikos, the whore who cries her wares from the rooftops and in the doorways. In the amazing Gnostic poem, *The Thunder, Perfect Mind*, she tells her own story:

> *I was sent forth from the Power*
> *and I have come to those who reflect on me . . .*
> *Do not be ignorant of me.*
> *For I am the first and the last.*
> *I am the honoured one and the scorned one.*
> *I am the whore and the holy one . . .*

I am the silence that is incomprehensible . . .
I am knowledge and ignorance.
I am shame and boldness . . .
I am war and peace . . .
I am the one whom they call Life
and you have called Death.
I am the one whom they call Law
and you have called Lawlessness . . .
I am the one whom you have scattered,
and you have gathered in together . . .
I am the knowledge of my inquiry,
and the finding of those who seek after me . . .
I am the substance and the one who has no substance.
What is inside you is what is outside of you
and the one who fashions you on the outside
is the one who shaped the inside of you.
And what you see outside of you, you see inside of you;
It is visible and it is your garment.

The paradoxes of duality lead through the teaching of
Sophia to the realisation of the mystery of union in which
the outer and the inner and the male and the female are
one. For Gnostics it is not so much actions that are
detrimental or sinful, but the loss of "Perfect Mind". What
the Gnostics seem to have meant by Perfect Mind is that
true self-knowledge which is lost through blind identification with the autonomous complexes.

Sex and individuation

Growth of consciousness begins with the keeping of
secrets and these secrets are often connected with sexuality. It is through sexuality that the feminine principle first
tries to awaken us to consciousness – and that is, the
meaning of Grace, which is one title of that Aphrodite
who is also Sophia.

Sexual secrets are amongst the first we learn to keep

from our parents and those in authority. In Egyptian mythology, the creation of the world is achieved through masturbation. The discovery of the secret garden is a numinous experience. Despite adult disapproval, veiled or explicit, the fruit tastes good and no dire consequences seem to result from its consumption. The solitary mysteries lead on to the quest for a partner, the Other, the soul-mate, the fulfilling counterpart. A new stage in the development of consciousness arises when the desired one is found. Inevitably, sooner or later, disillusionment sets in, and the greater the hopes, ideals, expectations and projections, the greater the disappointment. Whether disappointment leads to a renewed search or to settling down to make the best of a bad job, the myth of the 'right person' dies hard. Meanwhile, any relationship that survives beyond the honeymoon stage, as well as bringing the realisation that the beloved is not what one had expected, brings one face to face with the reality of one's own unacceptable dark side behind the shining mask, the shadow in our being. The acceptance of this and the attempt to come to terms with it is a life-time's work, but it is not the whole story. What of that longing for the unknown Other, whom nobody else quite seems to fit? When we realise that this contrasexual element is part of ourselves, a further opening up of consciousness becomes possible and we see that we have demanded so much of relationship that it has become a god, and inevitably, a god that fails. To seek relationship as an end in itself is to make of it a dead end.

A more conscious relationship is, paradoxically, one which leads to the discovery that one no longer needs the other person so much as one thought. Part of the Hera-script, the archetypal pattern of marriage, includes a regression to the primal dependency on the mother. As the infant's well-being depends totally on the mother, so the security of each partner comes to depend on the presence of the other. But the individuation process does not allow us to remain fixated forever in an unconscious attempt to recapitulate a paradisal pattern that probably never was, and one or other of the partners becomes alienated by such dependency. Then Hera brings forth her raging, jealous, vengeful monsters, and, after their devastations, a new pattern seeks to emerge, in which possessiveness yields to a mutual acceptance.

Thus disappointment and betrayal stimulate the need to withdraw projections and find one's meaning in one's own life, in which the partner is seen, no longer as an indispensable foundation on which all stands or falls, but as a phenomenon whom forces greater than the ego have attracted into one's own opus for furthering self-realisation.

What I have been describing is that dangerous thing, an ideal. For most of us, the so-called "individuation marriage"* in which every issue is confronted and made conscious, *sub specie aeternitatis*, is an idea whose time has not yet come. But the alternative is often a stultifying symbiosis, with each partner specialising in his or her strong points to the detriment of both partners' drive for self-fulfilment. In this model, which often to outsiders seems like the ideal marriage, the institution has devoured the individuals, and the self is submerged in the illusory world of "we", the grey limbo of pseudo-mutual coexistence.

But Hera, the binder and the bond, is also a sacrament, matrimony as materia. Pandora does, after all, keep one good gift hidden in the box, the cardinal, theological virtue of hope. Not the hope that two plus two will one day equal five, but the courage and confidence to connect with the possibility of ultimate meaning in life, that Hera will glorify Herakles; that the self-realising ego will be vindicated in its search for greater consciousness. The sin

* *Marriage Dead or Alive*, Adolf Guggenbühl, Craig Spring Publications, Zürich, (1977)

against the Holy Ghost in the depth psychology of Gnosticism would be to deny the reality of the principle of individuation operating in oneself and others as part of mysterious evolution within the cosmos. The microcosm reflects the macrocosm, and the logos in man is no different from the logos in the cosmos. The only law which must be obeyed is the law of one's own nature, a natural law, the spirit within nature. "Do not be antagonistic to the world of the senses," runs a Zen teaching, "for when you are not antagonistic to it, it turns out to be the same as complete Awakening."

Sophia encourages rebellion against the tyrant and seduces humanity along its evolutionary path, but the tyrant is still within us, and the process must be repeated in each life. Apart from his role as the great god Necessity in our inward parts, when he torments us with conflicting passions and instincts, the demiurge, as the personification of the collective, rules from within our institutions. We are all products of an educational system, class-structures, family and national prejudices and traditions, many forms of politicisation. The source of our being needs the demiurge which lives in ego-consciousness. It requires that he should become aware of the true source through relating in minute particulars to the reality of everyday life. Hera is not just marriage and the family, but those same institutions writ large in society with its contractual obligations. Money provides the best example of how the values of the collective are most forcibly expressed and it is no surprise to find that the very word stems from "Moneta", the Latin surname of Hera/Juno. But mother society has other and older means than money of establishing its binding norms. The greatest temptation for the wise child is to become a good boy or girl, selling out to collective values and his or her own desire to please mother, thereby betraying instinct, feeling, self-expression and, ultimately, self-preservation. So the need for approval leads to the formation of the persona, the compromise between society and oneself as to how one should appear to be.

But the father, too, has his norms and the consequences of the serpent's insidious advice have been terrible for the feminine principle, as the patriarchal consciousness of the ego has pursued its vendetta against it down through the centuries. The Church's war against the secret doctrines of the whore Wisdom began in the Epistles. Gnostic groups were sometimes led by women, so woman must be put down in the churches, and still is. "But I suffer not a woman to teach, nor to usurp authority over the man but to be in silence . . . Let the woman learn in silence with all subjection . . . notwithstanding she shall be saved in childbearing."* The murder by Christians of the Neo-Platonist teacher, Hypatia, in Alexandria, the destruction by crusade of the Cathar civilisation in southern France, the centuries of witch-hunts – these are just a visible sign of the deeply bigoted attitude towards the feminine that has marred the history of Christianity. The model of entelechy for women that the author of *I Timothy* proposed was childbearing and submission. The Germans have called it 'Kinder, Küche, Kirche'. In the Catholic world, salvation used to be assured through identification with Mary, either as virgin or sorrowing mother. Many signs now point towards the emergence of the feminine principle from its long passivity to activate a new mode of consciousness based on intuition and feeling. Entelechy, individuation – these are vague terms which do not define but suggestively and symbolically point in a certain direction towards an unknown destination. It is the fate of Gnostic writings to present themselves like a cross-word, or even a jigsaw puzzle, for the reader to assemble from clues and hints by dint of his own efforts and associations. Gnostics have their basis in consciousness that is not the ego's.

* *I Timothy*, II, 12–15.

Chapter 5

Lilith

WISDOM IN MOST languages is a feminine noun, often
personified as a woman or goddess: She is to be wooed,
attained or earned, prayed to and loved, may not be raped
or trifled with, though she loves to play. But where are
they now – Isis, Athene, Diotima, Hypatia, Sophia
herself? All, like Villon's ladies of former times, are gone
with the snows of yester year. Who today invokes Our
Lady as Seat of Wisdom or lights candles at the altar of St.
Catherine of Alexandria? So the voice of the eternal
feminine goes unheard and crying in the wilderness.

The wisdom of self-knowledge is the wisdom that
results from the union of conscious and unconscious,
masculine and feminine, within an individual – even
perhaps the marriage of heaven and hell.

When an image or motif constantly recurs in the dreams
of an individual it seems plausible to suggest that it
represents some content of the psyche which has been
repressed or ignored and demands to be acknowledged by
the dreamer so that it can find expression in his or her life.
It may be that a similar principle holds good on a collective
scale and that a one-sidedness in the dominant attitude of
western culture may be similarly detrimental to the
well-being of society. This would explain compensatory
"warnings" in the form of paranormal happenings such as
shared visions or hallucinations of a specific nature, almost
all involving the Blessed Virgin Mary, the equivalent in
Christian terms of the Great Goddess, that the world has

79

been receiving. Such manifestations have, in fact, been striking and frequent. It is as though something is trying to get through to us from the collective unconscious, and that something has to do with the feminine principle.

Between 1928 and 1972, for example, 232 apparitions of the Virgin attracted sufficient attention to be reported in the press and investigated by the church authorities. Some of these have given rise to important cults, though not yet on the scale of the great Marian shrines like Lourdes, Fatima, La Salette, Knock and others from the period 1830–1917. In the first few months of 1982 apparitions in the Auvergne and in Bosnia-Herzegovina attracted large crowds and some international attention, but, on the whole, such signs and wonders are treated as a nine days wonder and founder on the defences of our compartment psychology. One item of information which has failed to emerge even in the recent books* about the apparitions, which is relevant to our theme, is that, according to a well-informed source with access to Vatican archives, the Virgin in some of the apparitions was black.

Black is the colour of the unknown, the unconscious, and it is there that we must seek whatever it was that was repressed and lost long ages ago and now demands to be "found", redeemed and integrated. For this we must look at myths which date from, or look back to a time when, the feminine principle had not yet been subjugated to the structure of the patriarchy. Only in Mother India has the Great Goddess, never more potent than as the dark flame Kali-Lalita, retained her ancient prerogatives from time immemorial to the present day. It may be that the Aryan invaders found her already enthroned among the dark-skinned peoples of the Indus Valley civilization, which some authorities relate to that of the Chaldeans, but for us, in the West, it is to these inhabitants of Mesopotamia, and

* Colin-Simard, A. *Les Apparitions de la Vierge*, Fayard, (1981);
Chevalier & Gouley *Je Vous Salue Marie*, Fayard, (1981)

especially to their earliest predecessors, the Sumerians, that we must look for the origins of our myth and history at a time when the two were not sharply distinguished.

Images of the Goddess and what is said about her in the myths give some indication of the status of the feminine principle, and therefore of women, in the societies whence they derive. The oldest representations of the feminine form symbolize the power of fertility in innumerable small statuettes of stone or terracotta dating from the Old Stone Age to the Christian era. Sacred stones especially of meteoric origin and therefore dark in colour were no doubt the oldest forms under which such goddesses as Artemis, Cybele and Athene were worshipped, as well as furnishing the cult objects for oracles of the earth navel or cervix at Delphi and Paphos and the Islamic holy of holies, the stone of the Ka'aba of Mecca. A star-like object falls from the heavenly world of light to embed itself, darkened, in the earth, whence it is raised to be venerated as a source of life and a protective talisman, whose nature is androgynous or feminine. Likewise, in various religious traditions, an individual's starry essence falls through the planetary levels to become incarnate in a material body.

In Sumerian mythology of the third millennium BC the bright aspect of the feminine principle is represented by the Queen of Heaven, Inanna, who later develops into Ishtar, goddess of both the Morning and the Evening Star, the planet Venus, whereas the dark aspect is revered as Ereshkigal, redoubtable Queen of the Underworld. Inanna is a many-faceted figure, a potential universal goddess as all-embracing as Isis or Cybele were to be in the closing centuries of Hellenism. She is not just a fertility deity whose emblem is the ever replenished storehouse of the harvest home, but wields the double-axe symbol of earth and sky, matter and spirit. The harbinger of night and day, she presides over boundaries as ruler of fate and judge of god and man. She it is who bestows kingship over the land on her chosen one, and as goddess of battles, grants him victory. Accompanied by her lions and scorpions, she attacks like a storm, transcending the other gods as a falcon would a flock of sparrows. She even, most unusually for a goddess slays a dragon (but cf. St. Martha and St. Margaret). As goddess of love, she shows forth joyfully the active, uninhibited aspect of female sexuality. As patroness of the whole range of feminine wholeness, she is also the source of healing who sings the songs of creativity and life and presides over the gamut of human emotions. Although she is described as daughter and hierodule of the gods and has two sons who trim her nails, she is very much the virgin as one-in-herself rather than the player of some role in relation to the masculine, and when dispossessed by the new gods of the male ascendancy, she becomes a wanderer and laments to Enlil, her supplanter, the loss of her house:

I, the woman, who circles the land – tell me where
is my house . . . The bird has its nesting place, but
I – my young are dispersed.

This lament, echoed by the words of Christ, finds further parallels in the experiences of Inanna during the descent to the underground realm of Ereshkigal. As Sylvia Brinton Perera* writes of her:

Inanna's suffering, disrobing, humiliation, flagellation and death, the stations of her descent, her "crucifixion" on the underworld peg, and her resurrection, all prefigure Christ's passion and represent perhaps the first known archetypal image of the dying divinity whose sacrifice redeems the wasteland earth.

Inanna descends in order to attend the funeral rites of Gugulanna, the Bull of Heaven, who, in the Gilgamesh legend, appears as the goddess' own raging masculine destructive power. When she re-emerges, as Perera convincingly describes and amplifies, it is with a new

* *Descent to the Goddess*, Inner City Books, Toronto, 1981

rootedness in the law of her own instinctual-feeling nature. She has also integrated the dread Gorgon power of Ereshkigal to look with the "eye of death", even on her own careless lover, Dumuzi.

Inanna/Ishtar as an arthetypal image familiar to all has long since faded from consciousness, but there is one goddess with many of her attributes, dating from much the same period, who, in various guises, but generally recognizable and called by her own name, has remained remarkably alive and constant as an object of fascination and repulsion over the last 4,000 years, and that is Lilith. Part of Lilith's past is much bound up with Inanna/Ishtar, of whom she is in a sense a continuation. Inanna's throne is originally a three-fold tree not unlike Yggdrasil. At its roots lives a dragon and at its top a zu-bird, perhaps something like an eagle or stormy petrel, while, in the middle of the Huluppu tree, Lilith has her nest. When the hero Gilgamesh comes to slay the dragon and cut down the tree Lilith loses her home and becomes a wandering spirit and wailing djinn of the wilderness. She represents a very different influence for men and women, and it is particularly to men that she turns her seductive Ishtar face as part of a group of male and female demons, who as incubi and succubae arouse desire and have sexual intercourse with sleeping mortals.

Lilith's first appearance, on a Sumerian terracotta relief of about 1950 BC, known as the Burney relief, emphasises this role. She is represented as a beautiful naked woman with prominent breasts and sexual parts, standing on two lions, flanked by two owls, with a four-fold snake turban on her head and a pair of powerful vulture-like wings hanging from her shoulders. Her hands, raised as if in prayer, hold two objects that have been identified as a ring on a stick and likened to the sign for Libra or an ephah. Her gaze is impressively god-like and inscrutable when viewed straight on, though somewhat less formidable when seen from the side. Her least attractive features are the feet which consist of three hooked talons leading up to bird- or lizard-like corrugations around the ankles and a spur projecting below each knee. It is interesting to note the power of this image to constellate the dual role of Lilith for men and women in the differing reactions of Maria Teresa Colonna* who presents her in sharp focus head-on, and describes her as "the queen of death . . . impenetrable, severe, powerful, ineffable" with "two horrible birds", and Siegmund Hurwitz† who sees her as "extraordinarily beautiful . . . flanked by two naturalistic owls" and presents her in softened focus, slightly from the side.

For Lilith is, indeed, in her alternative role, like Artemis, a lion to women, especially in childbirth. As a terrible devouring anti-mother she comes prowling round the beds of women in labour, waiting to strangle the new born babes and suck their blood and bone marrow. An inscription of the seventh or eighth century BC shows her in this guise as a winged lion or sphinx and as a wolf with a scorpion's tail. This second aspect of Lilith derives, not from Inanna/Ishtar, but from the ancient Babylonian demoness, Lamashtu, who was expelled from heaven by her father An, the chief god, on account of her wickedness. Her name Lamashtu/Lamassu/Lamme probably lives on in the bisexual, child-stealing Lamias of Greece, and, indeed, Lilith is translated as Lamia in the *Vulgate* and the *Septuagint*. This image of the fallen, expelled feminine principle that turns negative and wreaks revenge on mothers and their children is of particular significance given the further development of the Lilith myth in Judaism and Gnosticism.

In this tradition, Lilith is Adam's first wife, created at the same time and of the same substance as he. She recognizes her full equality, and symbolizes it in her

* "Lilith or the Black Moon", *Journal of Analytical Psychology* (October 1980)

† *Lilith, die Erste Eva*, Daimon Verlag (1980)

demand that during sexual intercourse she should not always be expected to assume the inferior position. This leads to the first archetypal marital row, and Lilith becomes split off from Adam, cursed by God, and banished to the bottom of the Red Sea. There she brings forth myriads of demons and vents her jealous rage against Eve and all the children of Eve. Apart from killing the offspring of ordinary human wedlock she also had the power to prevent birth by barrenness, miscarriages and complications during childbirth. For this reason many Jewish homes from 600 AD up to recent times used to be protected by amulets or bowls inscribed with her various names or those of angels to ward off her evil influence.

Lilith's subsequent history within the context of Judaism showed a remarkable reversal of fortune. The twelfth-century Spanish Cabbalist, R. Isaac Hacohen, writes that "Lilith is a ladder on which one can ascend to the rungs of prophecy", and also connects her to the Tree of the Knowledge of Good and Evil. According to a later Cabbalist, Hayyim Vital (1543–1620), the angel called the flame of the revolving sword is, by night, Lilith. Similarly in Zoharic literature the Shekinah is at times called the mother and at times the Slave-Woman or Lilith. In another formulation, Lilith appears as the nakedness of the Shekinah during the time of Israel's exile. Lilith's greatest triumph is recorded in a sixteenth-century Cabbalistic writing where, as a result of a piece of divine wife-swapping, following the destruction of the Temple, God relinquishes his consort, the Matronit (identical with the Shekinah) to Samael/Satan and takes his queen, Lilith, to be his bride.

Such unlooked-for promotion of a relatively minor desert demoness of storm and darkness becomes more comprehensible when her intervening career is viewed through the eyes of Jewish esoteric exegesis. Not only did she succeed in having a child by the great prophet Elijah, and perhaps, as Zipporah, marrying Moses, but she actually, in her Hagar avatar, became the desert wife of the first patriarch Abraham, and ancestress of the Arab peoples. It may be thanks to this union that she was able to return one day from the deserts of the south in her most notable incarnation as the Queen of Sheba to test Solomon, the sacred King, builder of the Temple and personification of wisdom, with hard questions, and bear a son by him. Solomon had arranged a test for her, too, so that he could see beneath her skirts before she approached him. In one version she comes to a bridge across a stream but, recognizing it to be the wood from which the True Cross was to be made (naturally, since it was her own ancient home, the Tree of Knowledge of Good and Evil), prefers to hoist her skirts and wade through the water. In another version Solomon has a glass floor constructed in his throne-room to reveal her secrets.

The secrets are the animal and demonic nature of his visitor's nether members. They are, to begin with, unusually hairy, linking her with the hairy ones, the Se'ir, or desert djinns (and through the *langue des oiseaux* with those ominous starry wanderers, the comets). Solomon thoughtfully provides her with a special depilatory, and she is transformed to total comeliness. Sometimes it is the foot of a bird, goat or ass that she has acquired instead of one of her own, and again Solomon makes her whole. There is no need to spell out the Dionysian, diabolical, panic qualities associated with goatishness. Israel cast out the scapegoat and differentiated the beloved Jacob from the goatish Esau much as Christianity has always separated the sheep from the goats. The bird's foot, as we have seen, was already Lilith's attribute *ab initio*, and it links her to the swan-maidens and goose-queens of the west as well as to the host of harpies, sirens and demons of the night. The wild ass is also one of Lilith's own animals, and the steed of Lamashtu as well as being the beast of Saturn, planetary god of Israel and symbol of Set, the destructive Egyptian desert god. One Jewish exegete questions ironically whether the true Messiah would have ridden into Jerusalem on an ass if he had known the real nature of his mount.

The Queen of Sheba's visit to Solomon provides an important link in the continuum that runs from Lilith to the Black Virgins of Europe, through the refrain from *The Song of Songs*: "I am black but I am beautiful". For in the massive exchange of gifts between Solomon and the Queen, she departs with the two greatest gifts of all, Solomon's wisdom and the child that she will bear, Menelik, ancestor of the royal line of Ethiopia, on whom Solomon bestows the Ark of the Covenant. There may be a parallel to this legend in the recently revealed heretical secret that Mary Magdalene sailed to Provence after the Crucifixion bringing with her the wisdom of the feminine principle that was to blossom anew in Catharism and the cult of the Black Virgin in Southern France. Did she also carry, in the fruit of her womb, the holy blood of the King of Kings which is said to survive in the Merovingian line and provides one source of the Grail legends?* A further extrapolation of some piquancy concerns the latest and liveliest black religion to spring, seemingly spontaneously, out of the Judaeo-Christian matrix, Rastafarianism, in which the main cultic element is Ras Tafari, the Lion of Judah, the Emperor of Ethiopia.

To return to our main theme, according to Ethiopian legends, the one who is known to us as the Queen of Sheba was, as a girl, offered in sacrifice to a dragon that ravaged the land. She was tied to the branches of a tree for this purpose, and while awaiting her fate some of her tears (menstrual blood?) fell on to seven holy men who were resting in its shade. With their assistance she defeated the dragon, unscathed save for one foot touched by its blood which became transformed in the way that has been

* *The Holy Blood and the Holy Grail*, Baigent, Leigh and Lincoln, Jonathan Cape, London, 1982

described. The local people acclaimed her as a chieftainess and she went off to see if King Solomon could heal her foot. In a Jewish story Solomon is told by the hoopoe, who taught him the language of birds, about a land of which he knows nothing, the only part of the world not under his control. It is ruled by the Queen of Sheba, whom he then invites to come and visit him. This is an early example of that mysterious realm, ever in the golden age of Saturn, unknown to dominant masculine consciousness, where the feminine principle holds sway, that has furnished the theme of *She, L'Atlantide, The Lost Horizon, Perelandra*, Lothlorien in *The Lord of the Rings* and many another modern fantasy in which race memories of a matriarchal era are faintly echoed.

We have been moving away from Lilith in her negative aspects of terrible destroyer of mothers and babies or seductive anima, the *belle dame sans merci* who slays the lovers she chances on at the cross-roads. Her positive aspects relate particularly to the image of wisdom which comes from below, the ladder of the prophets, the ascent of the soul through the planetary stages and the uncoiling of Kundalini through the Chakras. For instance, one offspring of Lilith is that lowly but transformable creature, a frog. Rabbi Hanina, who hungered and thirsted for understanding of the *Torah*, was told by his father on his death-bed to go to market after seven days of mourning and buy the first article he found there, whatever the cost. This turned out to be a very expensive silver plate with another plate inside it containing a live frog. The Rabbi took it home and fed it so well that it grew vastly and needed a special room built for it. The frog taught him the *Torah* and the seventy languages of man as well as those of birds and beasts. It also took his wife into the forest and introduced her to all the animals, each of which brought her a precious stone and samples of the healing herbs and roots in whose virtues the frog instructed her. Before departing, the frog told the couple that it was engendered by Adam during the 130 years between the death of Abel and the birth of Seth, when he lived separately from Eve, and was receiving nocturnal visits from Lilith.

But it is above all in the *Ginza*, the sacred book of the Mandaean Gnostics whose descendants still survive in the swamps of the Tigris-Euphrates delta, a congenial setting for our wise frog, that Lilith's role as a wisdom figure, uniting heaven and hell, is best illustrated. According to Mandaeans, the underworld and its demonic denizens are under the dominance of Qin, the terrible mother of darkness. Her co-ruler is her daughter Ruha, the Mother of the Seven and of the Twelve. The brother/husbands seem to play a less prominent role. Another daughter of Qin mentioned in the Mandaean Book of John, is called Lilith-Zahriel, or Zahriel the Great. Either the great King of Light, Manda d'Hayye himself or his son Hibil-Ziva descend from the realm of light into the darkness to request from Qin and her husband Anatan, one of their daughters' hand in marriage. They give him their younger daughter, Lilith-Zahriel, from whom he learns the secrets of darkness and through whom he steals the objects on which the power and energy of the Kingdom depend, a magic mirror, a crown and a pearl. They ascend together to the Kingdom of Light and have a son called Ptahil, who possesses the wisdom of both realms, so that he can even answer the hard questions put to him by Kushta, the personification of the Way. He reveals that Lilith is no child-stealing demoness, but a good spirit, comforting women in labour and sitting beside them on their bed.

There are many analogues or possibly successors to Lilith to be found in the world's myths. Lamias and Empousas in Greece, as well as being nursery bogies, had the reputation for forcing their amorous attentions on men and then devouring them. The Sphinx is well-known for her perilous riddles and predilection for boys and youths, yet is hymned as the wise virgin. Sirens, mermaids, nixies, ondines, melusines and Rhine-maidens lure men into dangerous situations with their charms. All of them have, like Lilith, something inhuman about the lower half of their bodies, either fish- or fowl-like. Of flying demonesses, Harpies devour and pollute while the Furies pursue vengefully. The Gorgon Medusa and the Basilisk have, like Eresh-kigal and Inanna, the power to impose death with a look and share strong serpentine connections with the Hydra, the Echidna and the various dracs, dragons and wouivres (vipers/wyverns) of European folklore whose sites are very often close to those of the Black Virgins. Algol, the devil star, the Gorgon's head, was known in Hebrew astrology as Lilith. Scylla, the most terrifying of all these monsters has the face and breasts of a beautiful girl, while the lower part of her body consists of six devouring dogs or wolves with dolphin tails, the effect, according to Virgil, being that of a monstrous dragon. Less well-known is the Serpolnica of the Wends, a midday demon, covered in hair, with eyes of fire and pendulous breasts, who comes out of her lair between noon and two o'clock to put complicated questions especially about the growing and preparation of flax to young men still in the fields or wandering alone in the forest. If they fail to respond she rapes or kills them.

An interesting figure from the North African Arab tradition is Oumm es Sibyan or the Karina, who is described by King Solomon, evidently considered an authority on such matters, as an old grey-haired woman with blue eyes, eye-brows meeting in the middle (said to be a Scorpionic trait), sparse hair, thin limbs and an open mouth belching fire. Her speciality is to enter houses crowing like a cock and barking like a dog, braying like an ass, hissing like a serpent and carrying out various other animal imitations before completing her task of slipping into bed between a husband and wife making him impotent and sterile and her barren. Like Lilith, she pollutes the sperm, drinking the best of it and leaving the man with only a thin worthless liquid. She is called apotropaically "mother of children" because in fact she destroys them one after another in the same family. Roman creatures of the Lilith type were called Striges, 'screech-owls', and provide the derivation for 'strega', the Italian for witch. Incidentally, the only time Lilith is mentioned in the Bible, in Isaiah 34.14, her name is translated in the Authorized Version as 'screech-owl'.

It is curious that various strands of the Lilith tradition come together even nearer home in the folklore and customs of the French Pyrenees. St. Bertrand de Comminges, formerly the great city of Lugdunum Convenarum, situated between Lourdes to the west and the Cathar country to the east, was, according to Josephus, the place of exile where Herod Antipas and his wife Herodias, who engineered the beheading of John the Baptist, ended their days, accompanied, according to the Latin poet Rheismandus, by Salome. In the Middle Ages, the mother and daughter, condemned to wander endlessly in the night, combined in the figure, Nocticula, sovereign of the night, to preside over secret midnight assemblies, where amidst other excesses, children were sacrificed in fields of grass-cloth or wild flax, devoured, regurgitated and replaced in their cradles.

Nearby, in the Haute-Ariège, Denis Saurat recounted that, as recently as 1900, groups of eight to ten girls who came upon a young man from a different part of the country in a solitary place, would overpower him and use him for their amorous purposes.

Lourdes itself, white shrine of the Immaculate Conception, (the name she gave herself, unknown to the conscious mind of Bernadette), counterbalancing the ancient shrine of the Black Virgin of Aquitaine, Rocamadour, is not without its own dark and mysterious traditions long predating her apparition. According to one of these it was the great stronghold of Islam north of the Pyrenees and only yielded to Charlemagne in 778 AD when the Bishop of Le Puy, Rorice II, persuaded the Arab commander Mirat to accompany him to the shrine of the Black Virgin in his cathedral. There he was baptised Lorus, and his city was renamed Lourdes after him. Another legend recounts that when the Virgin Mary was evangelizing Gaul, she brought with her two pious Ethiopian maids, Tarbis and Lorda, who settled down between the mountains of the Bigorre and the plains of the Adour, giving their names to the two cities of Tarbes and Lourdes. An even older tradition relates to a war between Moses and Ethiopia, in which the Queen of that country fled to exile on the banks of the Adour.

It may be that such tales reflect traditions from Provence and Languedoc-Roussillon concerning Les Saintes Maries de la Mer and their dark Egyptian maid Sara, Martha and her dragon at Tarascon, and the Magdalen in her 30-year penitential solitude at Ste Baume, whom local tradition stubbornly links with Rennes le Château. Further speculation on such folkloric themes would, however, lead us too far afield. Certain historical facts, nevertheless, impose themselves. In 410 AD Alaric the King of the Visigoths captured and sacked Rome, possibly capturing the treasure of the Jerusalem Temple. Two years later the Visigoths had established themselves around Narbonne in the province of Septimania that was to remain theirs centuries after the rest of their possessions in Gaul had fallen to the Franks. There is some evidence that the city of Rhedae, on the present site of Rennes le Château, became the Visigoth capital. Certainly it was a very important stronghold from the beginning of the sixth century, in which the royal lines of the Visigoths and the Merovingians were linked. Some fifteen years before the proclamation of the Virgin Mary as the Mother of God at the Council of Ephesus in 431 AD, St. John Cassian left Egypt and established a shrine to St. Victor where Mary was venerated as Notre Dame de la Confession in the main cemetery of Marseilles, the Greek city where Artemis had reigned supreme for a thousand years. From there foundations for monks and nuns spread along the coastal areas where the Phocaeans had held sway, preceding by a century those of St. Benedict, usually considered the father of Western monasticism. A Jewish princedom based on Narbonne existed between 768 and 900 AD with the support of the Carolingian dynasty. By the early eleventh century Catharism reached France and flourished especially in Languedoc, Roussillon and Provence. The twelfth century saw the advent of a new order in Europe under the influence of the Cistercians and the Templars; thanks to the Crusades the Latin Kingdom of Jerusalem was established; the Gothic cathedral builders set about their task; pilgrim feet began to tread the various routes to Compostela, routes studded with Black Virgin shrines, whose miraculous statues of fabulous origin date from this period. St. Bernard of Clairvaux, credited by the Templars with founding the religion of the Virgin, is closely linked to all these phenomena.

There were from its earliest days influences alive in Christianity which gave far greater emphasis to the feminine principle in terms of belief, practice and organisation than has been acceptable to the Christian orthodoxies that have dominated Western culture up to the present day. Sometimes these influences were contained within the Church and modified by it, as in the cult of the Virgin Mary; sometimes they were branded heretical and extirpated, as was the case with Gnosticism, Catharism and witchcraft. For all practical purposes, the Church has remained since Constantine a rigidly masculine, hierarchical structure in whose organisation women have played little part. It thus perpetuated, in a way that vitiated its own inner meaning, the patriarchal spirit of Judaism, which had consigned Lilith to the bottom of the Red Sea. But even Jewish orthodoxy in its strictest periods never succeeded completely in eradicating the worship of the Goddess, who, as Lilith, was reinstated and honoured by the Cabbalists whose learning with that of the Arabs fed the culture of Languedoc.

Now that this archetypal presence is making itself ever more felt in our world, the need grows to make it as conscious as we can on its own archetypal psychological level. William Irwin Thompson writes movingly of the hockey match played by the men of Erech to celebrate the cutting down by Gilgamesh of Lilith's willow-tree home.* The game is watched by a young girl who feels totally excluded from this triumph of maleness, whom Thompson identifies as Lilith, the maid of desolation herself. She causes the earth to open and swallow up the puck. Enkidu, Gilgamesh's animal *alter ego*, attempts to retrieve it and is lost for ever in the underworld. When man excludes the feminine, he identifies with his Apollonian mind, and the instinctive nature turns shadowy. Dispossessed, Lilith turns into a little girl crying "it's not fair" and doing all she can to spoil the men's game. So down the ages she has made herself seductive to break up the one-sided and self-contained attitude of the all male hunting groups in their varying forms and avenge herself in devious ways for her dispossession and loss of integrity. Rivkah Schärf Kluger writes of the Queen of Sheba's hairiness as "a quality of displaced or unredeemed masculinity".† How was this masculinity displaced and how can it be redeemed?

Archaeological and mythological evidence shows how the great goddesses are dispossessed by the new gods of the Northern invaders and how representations of the Goddess change from powerful symbols of fertility to more ambivalent images, her dangerous strength hidden behind the masculine dream of the alluring houri. Thompson (op. cit.) adduces the archaeological evidence of Çatal Hüyük to postulate a period ending about 5400 BC in which women were the dominant sex in a gardening culture where customs and the religion of the Great

* *The Time Falling Bodies take to Light*, Rider/Hutchinson (1981)
† *Psyche and Bible*, Spring Publications (1974)

Mother ruled rather than the law of the warrior/hero/ king. It is likely that the Gilgamesh legend refers to a period at which intensive agriculture and the establishment of great cities, war and trade, replaced the smaller, horticultural townships of the Çatal Hüyük era. If this is the case, then, in terms of human evolution, the age of the equality or even dominance of the feminine principle is but yesterday, and Lilith is quite right to be grieving still at her dispossession.

Feminists are understandably suspicious of men who appear to espouse their cause, and I would not presume to do so. Based on my experience of working with women analysands, however, and in the interests of elucidating and interpreting the wail of Lilith, perhaps I may be permitted to stretch my imagination in an attempt to write a manifesto for the spirit of masculine protest and the disregarded and depreciated animus in women that I believe Lilith represents. In this I am encouraged by Plutarch's account of a mountain in India called Lilaeus which produces a stone of black colour called clitoris which the local inhabitants wear in their ears.*

Lilith is the consciousness of the absolute equality of male and female in the sight of God. This equality is reinforced by potential androgyny within each ("male and female created he them"), androgyny being a constant theme running through the tales relating to Lilith and her sisters. To make conscious the unconscious androgyny from whence we spring, so that each sex may express and realise itself through Eros and Logos, is the goal of human existence, the atonement, the *mysterium coniunctionis*, the *lapis*. Lilith and her sisters test masculine assumptions with hard questions ("typical animus manifestation"). Does he know about his own nature? Is he aware of the proto-alchemical process involved in the transformation of flax? What is the Holy Grail and whom does it serve? Can man

---

* A. Pertoka *Recherches sur le Symbolisme des Vierges Noires*, Zürich, 1974

justify his institutionalised rights over woman and her body?

Hard questions indeed. But Meridiana, the noon-day devil, has answers too, if man will woo her for her wisdom. Gerbert of Aurillac, alchemist, magician, inventor, possessor of a brazen talking head, found her across the Pyrenees, and from a shepherd-boy became the first Frenchman to ascend the throne of Peter, as Pope Sylvester II of the year 1000. St. Vincent de Paul seems to have encountered her too, near Rennes le Château, at Limoux, home, like Aurillac, of a famous black Virgin.

To those who fear her and scornfully shun her embraces she becomes accidie, the demoness of sloth and meaninglessness that John Cassian describes as afflicting the monks of the Thebaid. Without her blessing the waters of life dry up and wisdom desiccates into mere dusty, factual knowledge or airy theorising.

The howling desert storm demoness is also the Whore Wisdom, crying on rooftops, and the hairy repentant harlots and holy women like Mary Magdalen and Mary the Egyptian. Repentance is metanoia, change of mind, a stage in understanding that amounts to a transformation of habitual attitudes. Today the voice crying in the wilderness is Lilith's and, if we harden our hearts and refuse to hear, we seem likely to reap the whirlwind.

See also *Lilith ou la Mère Obscure*, Jacques Bril, Paris, 1981

Chapter 6

Wotan

MUCH HAS BEEN written in recent years of the repression of
the feminine principle. But the present world crisis
demands that we become conscious too of a wild restless
masculine spirit of aggressive expansion that today finds
little expression in the lives of individual men. The rituals
of manhood have largely disappeared, and, in consequence, the archetype of power is more unconscious and
more menacing than in the days of overt empire building
and unashamed national aggrandisement. The god who
best represents the repressed masculine craving for sup-
remacy is Wotan, so long eclipsed and misprised.

For men, power must be seen to be effective in the outer
world of the ego's goals and aims. But to become a "man
of power" in the shamanistic sense belongs more truly to
the essential nature of Wotan. In this mode strength is
demonstrated by the ability to work effectively with the
spiritual forces within the psyche. So let us now concern
ourselves with the archetype of power, whether it is
abused by tyrannizing others or directed towards gaining
the freedom to move at will in our inner worlds of choice.

It would seem from the Gospels that power belongs to
God and that those, like Pilate, who exercise it, would do
well to bear this fact in mind. On the other hand, power is
also in the gift of Satan and is his chief temptation.
Certainly the unbridled pursuit of power is one of the
greatest evils threatening the world today. With the advent
of nuclear weapons, our species would hardly survive

another Hitler, expressing and incarnating the collective power drive of a mighty nation. Such figures invariably arrogate to themselves the attributes of divinity and stifle the individuation process by usurping the position of the self for individuals within the societies they rule. They forge a spurious unity that is a mockery of integration by projecting the collective shadow on to imagined enemies at home or abroad. The dictator's subjects greet each other in his name and are urged to act always as if he were watching them, as indeed his image does from posters on every wall. Using lies, terror and corruption he sows disunity among those who oppose him, and offers the bait of advancement through co-operation to those who would share his power.

And lest any of us should be tempted to murmur "I thank thee, Lord, that I am not as other men are", I would recommend regular reading of Adolf Guggenbühl's *Power in the Helping Professions,** for all priests, analysts, doctors, social workers and teachers. Then too, as stewards of nature, men, and to some extent that is all of us, wield power unjustly and irresponsibly over the rest of creation, upsetting the balance of the species, denying to countless animals in our factory farms and laboratories any possibility of normal life, poisoning the earth and oceans, and sacrificing peace, beauty and wildness to the ever-increasing demands of technological progress.

Through the works of Castaneda and others, North Americans have come to appreciate, late in the day, the wisdom of the native culture that the advent of Europeans all but destroyed. This wisdom is based on the experiential knowledge that man is indeed the child of earth and starry heaven, with his own place as part of nature ordained by the great spirit. The Indian prays to the sun to assist it on its life-giving daily journey and learns about his own true nature from encounters with the night, the forests, the

* Spring Publications (1971)

animals and birds, the spirits of the ancestors and the beings that visit him in dreams. Part of this wisdom consists in not dividing the world and its contents up into the real and the imaginary, but according to everything its place in the imaginal realm of the soul in which everything has meaning.

Our Celtic and Teutonic ancestors of the old pagan forests would have had no difficulty in understanding and sympathizing with such an attitude since, broadly speaking, it was their own. The effect of an unresolved dualism at the heart of Christianity combined with the urban civilised ideal of Rome and Byzantium was to sunder man from nature, the body and the life of the instincts. A rare spiritual genius like St. Francis of Assisi went some way to redress the balance, but even he regretted having been on such poor terms with Brother Ass. To gain power over nature is the diabolical Faustian temptation to which western man has succumbed, and which has brought in its train the discontents of our civilisation, and it is a temptation to which males are particularly subject. Women have always been more aware of their own special inner power to bring forth and nourish new life and have, in consequence, less urge to stamp their mark on the face of the world. The equivalent for men might be to allow the birth of soul to take place within them.

There was a time, though, in the twelfth and thirteenth centuries, when, enriched by the dying efflorescence of Celtic culture, Christianity, art and nature, the masculine and the feminine, walked hand in hand. One factor in this harmony was the archetypal wizard Merlin, the offspring of the Devil and a pure virgin, gifted with knowledge of past and future and the secrets of nature. He was the hidden inspirer of the whole ideal of Arthurian chivalry, and its literary expression in the late middle ages, especially that period of the courts of love and the great cathedrals in honour of Our Lady, when the feminine principle flowered in the Gothic renaissance. For a time priests and true servants of the Church like St. Albertus Magnus were also the great scientists, alchemists, astrologers and mages. Then all was shattered and split once again: the Church of Amor separated itself from that of Roma and the Albigensian crusade was unleashed for its destruction: womanhood throughout Europe was degraded and denigrated by centuries of witchcraft trials, while, concomitantly, the use of the natural intuitive powers and their development became increasingly subject to suspicion and repression.

In their book *The Grail Legend*,* Emma Jung and Marie-Louise von Franz draw attention to the similarities between Merlin and Wotan: "In Merlin the older image of God is probably resuscitated, an image in which aspects of Wotan are mingled with the archetypally related Kerunnus, an image of inner wholeness which still presses its unfulfilled claims on man."

According to James Hillman† the repressed gods return as the archetypal core of sympton complexes, and Wotan has suffered a triple repression. The first was when the Teutonic tribes, some of them, like the Goths and Lombards, even named after Wotan, poured across the Rhine and the Danube to seize the spoils of the Roman Empire and emerge as the new Herrenvolk. As though ashamed of the untamed and primitive nature of the chief of their pantheon, they assumed the religion of those they had conquered, one singularly unfitted for a wild warrior race at the apogee of its triumph.

In the heartland itself, conversion was slower, and was generally the result of rulers imposing Christianity on their subjects. As late as the end of the eighth century, Charlemagne was struggling to force the Cross on the obdurate Saxons after a thirty years war of conversion by terror, massacre and deportation. In this war the myste-

---

* Hodder and Stoughton (1971)

† *Pan and the Nightmare*, Spring Publications (1972)

rious Irminsul, Wotan's "column of the world" which stood in a sacred grove near Marsberg was destroyed by Charlemagne. In some parts of Scandinavia and in Iceland the old religion was not extirpated until well on in the eleventh century. Of all the Teutonic gods none was considered more dangerous to the priests and missionaries than Wotan and none was more thoroughly repressed. In Germany he was even effaced from the calendar so that his day, from "Wotanstag", became "Mittwoch". The meal of communion with Wotan in which the flesh of his totemic animal, the horse, was ritually consumed, was so effectively repressed that the idea of eating horse is still an abomination to most of our fellow-countrymen.

The Greek and Roman gods lived out their lives and possibilities, were reincarnated in the saints, angels and divine attributes of the Christian era and throve under their own names in alchemy, astrology and all the arts of the Renaissance. For the gods of the North, on the contrary, rebirth had to be preceded by the last battle, Ragnarok, and the Götterdämmerung.

Of Wotan's second eclipse, when Merlin, the Grail and Arthur went underground, or into hiding in the forests, perhaps to return one day, we have already spoken. He was never, like Thor, the God of Norwegian and Icelandic farmers, but of the Kings and warriors of mainland Europe, and his last real stronghold was Denmark. He appeared in a vision to the most rabidly Christianising Danish King and proposed a deal – the new and old religions could co-exist peacefully with a view to a possible merger, instead of fighting each other. He was, of course, negotiating from a position of weakness and had in any case a notorious reputation for trickiness and treacherous behaviour, so he was turned down. He lingered on, disguised in place-names, fairy tales and folk traditions such as Robin Hood – one of his English names, Grim, can mean 'a mask' – sallying forth occasionally to counter-attack the usurper, as when he invaded and captured

Christmas and emerged as Faust's Mephisto. But on the whole he remained thoroughly unconscious, going bad and raising a stink as the violent shadow of northern European Christianity. When he reappeared on the scene with Wagner and the reunification of Germany, it was to be in his most negative form of Furor Teutonicus and Lord of the Berserkers, and it was probably too late to integrate him into the collective consciousness of the most cultured and orderly nation on earth. Nietzsche attempted to assimilate him as Dionysos or Zarathustra but suffered instead a possession that led to madness and death. Wotan and his people now demanded the long-delayed place in the sun that their talents merited. In 1914, ninety-three German intellectuals signed a "Manifesto to the Civilized World" declaring that German culture and German militarism were inseparable – love me, love my dog. Wotan's battle-fury did not blow itself out with the four years of the Great War. With the advent of Hitler it became indeed explicit, and the old God was once again invoked in the frenzied litany of "Sieg Heil!" Since 1945 we have seen neither hair nor hide of him in his old stamping grounds. It may be that, like so many of his votaries he has emigrated and now dwells among the Teutons of the diaspora. Violence is, after all, as American as cherry-pie, and God's own country would, perforce, cast a dark shadow. The conscious idealism of America was shattered by the trauma of Vietnam. If the Wotanic nightmare of recent years can now be allowed to heal through acceptance and self-forgiveness then much will have been done to appease the wrath of the god.

For Wotan is not just violence. Jung describes him as: "not only a god of rage and frenzy who embodies the instinctual and emotional aspect of the unconscious. Its intuitive and inspiring side also manifests itself in him, for he understands the runes and can interpret fate."* Can it be

* *Collected Works*, Vol. 10, Routledge & Kegan Paul Plc (1954)

that he is the secret shamanistic patron of depth psychology, whose sacred texts are in the German tongue? Jung continues: "Wotan must, in time, reveal not only the restless, violent, stormy side of his character, but also his ecstatic and mantic qualities . . . Things must be concealed in the background which we cannot imagine at present, but we may expect them to appear in the course of the next few years or decades."

We need a renewed and transformed image of the Wotan archetype and a sketch for the sort of inner saviour figure one might expect to inspire our own new age and we need to see where and how he is manifesting himself. Colin Wilson, a writer who generally keeps well in touch with the zeitgeist, writes in *The Occult** of the supersensory faculties which he claims are possessed by at least 5% of human beings, and states that in their development lies the possibility of achieving the next stage in evolution. It seems plausible that contact with the hidden imaginative and intuitive powers of one's own psyche could prove more durable as a satisfaction than the exercise of power over others. It is the fascination of such a quest that drives people to risk death and madness in the use of mind-expanding drugs, though I believe that in using such means they are misguided. Wotan is an intoxicator, but only those for whom his hydromel is intended can use it to reach the stage of illumination. Some gets slopped over the edge of the vessel, and the fool-poets who drink it up are possessed, deluded and humiliated thereby. But it is not only in blowing the mind with narcotics that Wotan seeks to return to consciousness. He reveals himself in the wanderlust, the yearning for return to the forest and wild nature, anarchy and the casting-off of all bonds, and in unconventional and uninhibited sexuality.

It is regrettable that ancient Teutonic astrology through which Wotan and his fellow deities played their part in the

* Hodder and Stoughton (1971)

celestial sphere, is now almost wholly lost to us, for astrology is one way of keeping an eye on the gods. In terms of our Greek-based astrology, Wotan has clearly much in common with many of the planets – Mercury, whose day he shares; Mars, as god of war; Jupiter, as all-seeing father; Neptune, through alcohol, illusion and mysticism; Pluto, in his connection to the underworld. But Wotan's closest affinity seems to be with the planetary god of magic, inspiration and sudden change – Uranus.

Many astrologers believe that of the twin rulers of Aquarius, Saturn and Uranus, Uranus is more in harmony with what is known of the sign. This is curious, because very little is related of Uranus in mythology beyond the notion that he was a sky-god wedded to earth who hid his children in her depths, and was eventually castrated by one of them, Kronos/Saturn. After this, like most sky-gods, he was more or less neglected and received little cultic or literary attention. The astrological Uranus, on the other hand, is a very different figure: his discovery between the American and French revolutions makes him, naturally, something of a rebel, and the technological breakthroughs that date from his time explain his interest in scientific inventions. But where did Gustav Holst get the idea that Uranus was a magician, and why did Alan Leo, writing in the early years of the century, assert that it was "the planet of the coming race, governing whatever is original, eccentric, and free to act apart from any conventional groove or accepted custom, the planet of regeneration?"

There does seem to be a considerable element of fantasy or projection in the astrological view of Uranus, over and above what could have been gleaned from mythology or the objective experience of a few generations' horoscopes. The result bears a striking similarity to what we know of that master of disguises and surprises, Wotan, in his sky-god aspect, and as Mephisophelean granter of wishes at a price. Even the latest tendency, derived possibly from the Tarot, to depict Aquarius as a beautiful woman, fits the sexual ambiguity attributed to Uranus and accords with Wotan's proclivities for changing sex as often as he changes form.

We should not imagine that a discarded deity like Wotan has nothing to do with this world and its problems. If the irrational is repressed and finds no place in our scheme of things it explodes dangerously in inferior and negative ways as the collective shadow. Memory of Wotan's last two eruptions should at least encourage us to take seriously the possibility of a third. The danger of repressed Wotanic fury breaking out in the form of world nuclear war is an ever-present possibility while mutual shadow projection lies at the root of foreign policy. The ways in which repressed Wotan has manifested himself most characteristically since the second world war has, however, been through shadow projection within individual societies. Wotan is a sower of discord and must find the urban guerrilla warfare of Belfast and so many other cities and countries entirely to his satisfaction. If we can strive to understand and integrate our own Wotanic shadows, fostering, instead of criticizing, any of the positive ways in which the long-repressed behaviour pattern that I have referred to as Wotan may be trying to express itself, the voice that whispers "Hope" amid the destruction of Ragnarok, may yet prove valid.

How can we envisage, or envision, a new dispensation in which Wotan returns transformed and whitened from immersion in Mimir's well? If, from his house in Gladsheim, not one of the zodiacal signs but the circumpolar constellations of the Bears, the Old Eagle still looks down wakefully on the events of middle-earth, or sends his ravens to spy the land, has he a good spell for us? All-father, wide in wisdom, the truthful one, wand-bearer and wanderer, god of countless names, his association with the pole, the spear and the world-tree point us to the spine with its different centres of energy and consciousness. Wotan as "The Changing", who can assume any shape, who exists as eagle, stag and corpse-eating serpent at different levels of Yggdrasil, as well as the squirrel Ratatosk who runs up and down between them all, reminds us of the multi-faceted nature of consciousness, and of the many modes potentially accessible to us. When we invoke him as "Way-weary" we acknowledge his understanding of those toiling on the path of individuation. But Wotan, "The Much-Loved", is no god of kill-joys and puritans. He himself takes no nourishment other than wine, giving all on his plate to his two wolves, and those who are with him never suffer from a hangover, however much they drink. It is said in one of the sagas that when he was sitting among his friends his countenance was so beautiful and dignified that the spirits of all were exhilarated by it. As chief of the poets, he speaks everything in rhyme, and since it is as a bird that he steals the mead of inspiration, we may be sure that his speech is the riddling, enigmatic, subtle minstrelsy of bards and troubadours, true on many levels, that some call the "langue des oiseaux" but which is also the logos of the psyche.

Conclusion

WE CAN CHOOSE not to be wholly confined within the stale predictability of ego consciousness. Perhaps our freedom of will consists in this – a flexibility to manoeuvre between one fantasy, one channel of energy, and another. It is unfortunate that our thinking and talking about this has been conducted mainly in binary ego terms. According to this principle, there is the ego's mode of functioning, or there is something mysterious called the 'unconscious' which is what we are in when the ego is not functioning. Everything is black or white. Admittedly, when the sun is shining we are not aware of the darkness, but are there not many nuances of daylight – dawning, dusky, misty, grey, and, in the mind, twilight states, dreams of sleeping and waking, cloudy consciousness, the catatonic state from which the patient may emerge with total recall of all that took place? Just as we can differentiate between degrees of cloud-cover during the day, so we are aware that the night is not wholly dark. The moon comes and goes, planets and the first bright stars emerge, and, if we watch long enough, groups of stars form themselves into the familiar constellations before our eyes.

Using this analogy, why should we consider it an adequate account of human experience to insist that the fine and subtle shadings of the mind's perceptions should be placed so arbitrarily under the rubrics of "conscious" or "unconscious"? Must it always be a question either of having an integrated animus, i.e. assimilated by the ego, or of being animus-possessed? Our signature is in all we do and our identity is stamped on every cell of the body, but it is not the ego's signature or character. The ego may, in the revitalisation it undergoes through its experience of the other contents of the psyche, become the exponent of the self, and operate without loss of integrity in many archetypal modes, but it does not become the self.

When Herakles reports back from each of his labours, he is not allowed to approach too closely to King Eurystheus, though at death he is united to the true source of his trials and his glory, Hera. In one of the Gnostic myths, Sabaoth, an inferior archon, hears the voice of Sophia, loves it and is taken up to be with her, beyond the planetary spheres. This is the ego won over to the service of entelechy. But another of the archons dissembles, pretending to love compassionate wisdom, but secretly hating it. This warns us of the ego's tendency to take over everything, including the principle of individuation, and use it as grist for its own mill, to further its own ends.

Depth psychology, when it remembers its immediate origins in medical psychotherapy, is obsessed with the need to build up and preserve the integrity of the poor, weak ego. If only it remembered the roots it has in religion, it would realise that the problem for most people is the almost invincible strength of the ego-persona system, entrenched behind its defences, effortlessly proving to itself that it is the only god, infallible and omniscient. I suspect that the majority of people undergoing analysis today could in no strictly medical sense be diagnosed as ill, but suffer from mal de siècle, the meaninglessness that comes from restriction to the world of ego and its discontents.

The ego is just one channel through which energy – like consciousness, another word that we do not understand – flows from its unknown source into manifestation. Freedom and refreshment for our essential nature are to be found in new impressions that slip past the network of ego-associations to fall on an unrealised potentiality and awaken it to life, so that we experience ourselves and the world in a new way.

The incoming energy stimulates the energy within the organism. The term 'energy' to the Greeks was closely allied to the concept of entelechy in its sense of actualisation of the life-force, and is opposed in meaning to "habit" and "potentiality". Blake called it "eternal delight", and, to the classical world, entelecheia, absoluteness, completeness-in-itself, actual being, was linked with endelecheia, perennial being, eternity. The eternal, creative, first thought of God, who "was daily his delight", leaps forth to energize the chaotic potentia, and finds her "delight with the sons of men". The energy knows where it wants to go but needs the co-operation of human consciousness for self-actualisation. There are many modes and movements through which the vital force may express itself in its attempt to realise the final cause. A privileged and basic one is the Aphrodite mode of consciousness which sends the soul on its love-trip, life's adventure, in which the goddess delights to play hide-and-seek with herself.

Extraversion, introversion, thought, feeling, sensation and intuition, the humours, the elements, the planets and the signs of the zodiac, all are theophanies, modes through which the unknown may reveal itself. The spontaneous, living word of mercurial communication, which makes each sentence a voyage of self-exploration on an uncharted course, is how the logos mode appears when the ego is no longer in complete control. How do I know what I think until I see what I say? The mode of Saturn, with its leaden despair, may, if we brood on it and work with it, yield to our patience the philosphers' gold of psychic transformation. For those too ego-bound, the wine of Dionysos, the loosener, may provide a means to divorce old, barren reason from their beds and become poets for an hour or two.

For this chameleon-like adaptability to be realised, the ego would have to forgo its tendency to hog the stage with its own habitual act and be prepared to slide, slightly out of control, in the direction the energy wants to take. Instead of being a one-man band, it could become the impresario and compère of a phantasmagoric variety show. Pico della Mirandola saw man as containing seeds of all kinds and free to cultivate which he will – vegetative, rational or intellectual, "and if, happy in the lot of no created thing, he withdraws into the centre of his own unity, his spirit, made one with God, shall surpass them all . . . who would not admire this our chameleon?"*

Of the unknown source and goal of energy, to which, I take it, Pico is referring, the self, there is nothing to be said and I shall not attempt to say it. Its presence may be hinted at in dreams, visionary states, paranormal happenings and synchronicities, but the experience is one thing and one's interpretation of it, coloured by conditioning, associations and the language of everyday life, inevitably another. The new wine is all too often poured into old bottles and spoiled.

There is no Richter scale for measuring the intensity of numinous experience, but people who have undergone an encounter with the "wholly other" are powerfully affected by it, whatever language they use, and frequently find their lives and sense of identity transformed as a result. Abraham Maslow's work[†] has emphasised the positive effects of "peak-experiences" and shown how their setting can often be everyday and humdrum. Sir Alister Hardy's religious experience research unit at Oxford[‡] testifies to the importance of such experiences, often called mystical,

* "Oration on the Dignity of Man", translated by Elizabeth Livermoore Forbes in *The Renaissance Philosophy of Man*, ed. Ernst Cassirer, University of Chicago Press

[†] *Towards a Psychology of Being*, Abraham H. Maslow, van Nostrand Insight Books, New York (1962)

[‡] *The Biology of God*, Sir Alister Hardy, Ch. 10, London (1975)

throughout all sectors of the population. The findings suggest that this mode of consciousness forms a vital part of the treasure-store of "normal" people. It is, I think, a measure of the power of the ruler of this world and the dominance of ego-consciousness that so few people dare to admit publicly to having had such an experience, which is the heritage of us all.

To talk of such experiences is always to risk diminishing their value. It seems, nevertheless, as we distance ourselves from the Piscean pendulum-swing between self-indulgence and remorse, that the possibility of entering the Kingdom of Heaven through not doing what we hate may become less reprehensible. By extension, doing what brings us the joy of a peak experience may come to be regarded as healthy, in the sense of conducive to whole-ness, and even respectable. (Though, of course, Piscean mysticism would be right in reminding us that spiritual consolations belong to the realm of grace, a state of consciousness beyond that of our ego's willing and striving.)

If our world and we, the individuals who inhabit it, are not to remain forever crucified between those two thieves, the opposites, our hope must lie in the non-rational third thing which is not given, the alchemical *solutio* or dramatic *lysis* – two terms redolent of Dionysian paradoxy – in which the goose flies the bottle and the sound of one hand clapping drowns out the constant moaning of problems from the binary world. How we love those insoluble problems of God and the Devil, of a good pursued to the point of evil and evil done in the name of good!

There is indeed a mystery of evil abroad in the world, and a deep shadow in the depths of every human soul. Now may be the right time, the kairos, to reflect on Christ's injunction "that ye resist not evil", and consider how to practise it as a psychological attitude. That this is not just a piece of Christian wetness is attested by St. Paul's commentary in *Romans* XII, 20 that "in so doing thou shalt heap coals of fire on his head", an effective piece of spiritual judo, but only if it comes from the right place: beyond, above, below or between the opposites. Apotropaic deterrents are one thing, but coals of fire may prove somewhat excessive for foes without and especially those within, when we realise, on our individual or collective battlefield of Kuruk-shetra, that it is ourselves that we are fighting.